An In

Chu

Multicultural

World

An Intercultural Church for a Multicultural World

REFLECTIONS ON GIFT EXCHANGE

Martyn Snow

With contributions from

Lusa Nsenga-Ngoyo, Saju Muthalaly,
Florence Gildea & Jessie Tang

© Martyn Snow 2024

Church House Publishing
Church House
27 Great Smith Street
London SW1P 3AZ

Published 2024 by Church House Publishing

The opinions expressed in this book are those of the author and contributors and do not necessarily reflect the official policy of the General Synod or the Archbishops' Council of the Church of England.

British Library Cataloguing in Publication Data

A catalogue record for this book is available from the British Library

ISBN 978 1 78140 472 0

Printed and bound by CPI Group (UK) Ltd, Croydon, CR0 4YY

Contents

Abbreviations

BAME	Black, Asian, Minority Ethnic
EDI	equality, diversity and inclusion
GMH	Global Majority Heritage
IWC	Intercultural Worshipping Community
UKME	United Kingdom Minority Ethnic
GMH	Global Majority Heritage

Foreword

By Bishop Lusa Nsenga-Ngoy

'Timeo Danaos et dona ferentes.' 'Beware of the Greeks even when bearing gifts.' This Latin adage from Virgil's epic poem, the *Aeneid*, an echo from my school years, occasionally resurfaces with some washed-out wisdom about weariness in my engagement with others, particularly when those are not people I share affiliation and affinity with.

The story behind the maxim has often served as a cautionary tale towards outsiders coming with ploy and subterfuges, intent to saw destruction. This and similar narratives have socialized and inducted us into liturgies of suspicion where the other – the stranger – is to be, at best, feared and, often, persecuted.

The polarized and often toxic political landscape in Britain, particularly in its vehement problematizing of migrants in political discourse and policies, well illustrates that point. We are left with exacerbated tensions and fractures between communities. Our weariness of the other precludes us from fostering the kind of relationships that would enable mutual flourishing and harmony. Instead, we are left with a legacy of mistrust and distrust in which any exchange proves costly. And in such a context, the cost in the exchange is often asymmetrically borne between the giver and the receiver.

When, in September 2017, I arrived in the Diocese of Leicester to serve as the BAME (Black, Asian, Minority Ethnic) Mission and Ministry Enabler, I had a clear sense of what my brief was: help develop our confidence and competence as a diocese in mission and ministry to and for those whose heritage was traced beyond the British Isles.

My primary task was to focus on the development of two distinctive initiatives, aimed at tending to the needs of two of the main allochthone communities in Leicester, namely the African Caribbean and the South Asian communities.

As I travelled around Leicester and Leicestershire, I soon realized that, typically, churches did not reflect the breadth of diversity held within their wider community setting. Though there was an advertised longing for greater inclusion of UKME (United Kingdom Minority Ethnic) Christians in the life, structures, and governance of the church at parochial and diocesan levels, the lived experience offered a contrasting reality.

What I encountered in Leicester was far from being a singular experience within the Church of England. English Anglicanism seemed defined around an implicit and often uncomfortable axiom about identity and belonging predicated on the imperative of assimilation to a set of normative cultural, socio-economic, ethnic and linguistic norms.

This tyranny of assimilation has become an invisible line of demarcation between hospitality and hostility in our church's engagement with those whose cultural, ethnic, linguistic and socio-economic heritage does not neatly align with our normative narratives. To paraphrase Dr Martin Luther King Jr, 'the worship hour seems indeed the most segregated hour of the week in Christian Britain'.

However, it became evident, in conversations with many Anglicans of global majority heritage, as well as with several white British sisters and brothers in Leicester, that the vision of a segregated expression of the church left many of us deeply unsatisfied. Instead, I heard the articulation of a vision of the church that would intentionally resist the seduction of homogeneity and commit to curating spaces of mutuality and belonging; where we would learn from and with one another new ways of speaking of God, of worshipping, of inhabiting societal and historical fault lines, and naming one another's reality, committed to 'walk the mile and bear the load' for each other.

This aspiration was a compelling call beyond the politically charged notions of equality, diversity and inclusion (EDI). It was a commitment to foster belonging as our ultimate quest, learning to discern and discover that the other was a gift to be treasured and celebrated; occasionally realizing that we too could be that other; we too could be the gift. Though we did not quite have the language to express it, what started to emerge in our shared aspiration was the intuition that there was a better way of being church together, there was a better way to follow Jesus Christ.

Soon we discovered that the intuited reality had a name, a posture, a rhythm and a set of liberative practices echoing with the biblical imperative of a world reconciled across all its fractures and gathered in worship before God. This vision we called the Intercultural Worshipping Community (IWC).

To live interculturally is to be introduced to a new hermeneutical lens that resets and reorientates norms and values not merely towards a new way of thinking, but an altogether transformed way of living, doing and being in the world. That required the commitment to unlearn established patterns of living and espouse a new nomenclature of faith and self-definition from estrangement to embrace, from dispersion to congregation, from segregation to integration. In the process, we gained a sense of fluency in the intercultural vernacular, acquiring cultural humility and its power to liberate often hidden and marginalized human stories.

Intercultural living comes with a complex and rugged topography. It is not concerned with reductionist imperatives. Instead, it compels one to lean into the tension of nuance and paradox, to embrace complexity and resist simplistic and essentialising narratives. It is less about finding and exploiting the lowest common denominator and more about seeking the highest common multiple. As such, the intercultural frame is about expansion, not contraction. It constantly invites us to lift our gaze to a horizon that we soon realize is open towards God's future, a future where mutual flourishing can be our lived reality. In that space, we are freed from the anxiety of betrayal and exploitation and afforded an opportunity to redefine our human stories beyond fracture and dispersion as we retell a hopeful version of our shared story.

In her beautiful poem 'The Speed of Darkness', Muriel Rukeyser suggests that 'The universe is made of stories, not of atoms'. This is a thought echoed in many global cultures. The stories we tell about ourselves, each other, the world and our vision for the future, all help form the people we become. Stories enable us to navigate the world. They induce meaning and inference. They nurture and release our hope.

At a time when the politics of fragmentation are gaining currency, Bishop Martyn Snow offers an opportune invitation to resist simplistic discourses and enter a complex, perplexing and paradoxical universe where we are afforded the opportunity to retell and redeem our formative stories. Like an African griot, he draws us into a new story, not merely as spectators, but as artisans of new narratives that will enable the emergence of new communities and ultimately a new humanity inexorably compelled to articulate its identity in interdependence.

When we embarked on this journey with colleagues and friends in Leicester Diocese, little did we anticipate that what began as tentative steps in a new direction would quickly become a radically life-altering event. In the process, we discovered ourselves companions on the journey and followers of Jesus Christ, the ultimate reconciler of cultures.

For me, the intercultural landscape has become more than a conceptual notion to be explained. It is a reality to be lived. For the intercultural reality is one that is embodied, incorporated. It is best translated in the altered accentuations of our respective narratives, especially when we enable our respective stories to collide and intersect with the other's. In the process, we realize that this is the heart of the incarnation, God who in Christ enables the divine story of salvation to intersect with our stories of perdition. The intercultural ethos is an invitation to depart from the shores of Troy, to migrate from xenophobia to xenophilia; from the anxiety of kingdom building to the opportunity of fostering God's peaceable kin-dom. It is a call to shift from othering to 'one anothering'.

The Rt Revd Lusa Nsenga-Ngoy

Bishop of Willesden

1. Introduction

On 4 August 1972, the military dictator of Uganda, Idi Amin, announced that all Asian people who were not Ugandan citizens would be given 90 days to leave the country. Over 60,000 Ugandan Asians were forced out. Around 27,000 with British passports came to the UK, many of whom settled in Leicester.

Nisha Poppat was one of them. She was 12 years old and remembers the serenity of life in Uganda, climbing mango trees while her family picnicked under the warm African sun. But their lives were rudely interrupted when the President made his announcement. Together with her younger brother and three older sisters, she travelled to the UK. Her parents joined them four weeks later. 'Part of me felt it was like an adventure and I think I didn't totally grasp that this would be home. My mum kind of made it out to be, "You're going on holiday – you're going to have a good time."'

Uganda's ruler, Idi Amin, had found a convenient scapegoat for the country's economic ills in the form of the Asian community, whom he openly accused of 'sabotaging the economy of this country'. Amin was also aware of rising anti-immigrant sentiment in the UK and saw an opportunity to pay back his critics. Just a few years earlier, Enoch Powell had prophesied 'rivers of blood' brought about by immigration. And in 1972, speaking of the Ugandan Asians, the hero of Britain's anti-immigrant Right declared, 'Their so-called British passports do not entitle them to enter Britain.'

The exiles therefore found themselves between three countries that did not want them: they faced expulsion from their homes in Uganda; the Indian government wanted no role in the matter; and the British people were split in their views. Nevertheless, 27,000 were allowed to enter the UK through a quota system (Canada also took some of those seeking asylum, as did the United States and Germany).

Yet even once this decision had been made, Leicester City Council took out adverts in Ugandan newspapers. They read:

The City Council of Leicester, England believe that many families in Uganda are considering moving to Leicester. If YOU are thinking of doing so, it is very important that you should know that PRESENT CONDITIONS IN THE CITY ARE VERY DIFFERENT FROM THOSE MET BY EARLIER SETTLERS. They are:–

HOUSING – several thousands of families are already on the Council's waiting list

EDUCATION – hundreds of children are awaiting places in schools

SOCIAL AND HEALTH SERVICES – already stretched to the limit

IN YOUR OWN INTERESTS AND THOSE OF YOUR FAMILY YOU SHOULD ACCEPT THE ADVICE OF THE UGANDA RESETTLEMENT BOARD AND NOT COME TO LEICESTER[1]

The advert backfired as many people who had not heard of Leicester decided to come! Nisha Poppat was one of these, and in 2022 she curated an exhibition in Leicester: *Rebuilding Lives: 50 Years of Ugandan Asians in Leicester*. The exhibition won a prestigious Museum + Heritage award, beating the National Trust and the big museums of London.

Quite a turnaround for someone who fled her home country and received racist abuse on her arrival in the UK.

Migration and diversity are here to stay

The arrival of Ugandan Asians in Leicester was the beginning of the transformation of the city. Forty years later (around 2012), following further significant immigration, the white British population of Leicester became a minority, with South Asians or Asian British as the majority group. Leicester is not unique in this regard – several London boroughs and places like Slough, Luton and Bradford have similar demographics. While population predictions for the future can only be tentative, most specialists agree it is likely that diversity in the UK will continue to grow.

On 3 June 2023 an article appeared on the BBC homepage entitled *'Former home secretaries on why it's so hard to cut migration'*. The article, by Laura Kuenssberg, was written following interviews with five former Home Secretaries of both Conservative and Labour governments. It was published in the context of the highest ever net migration figures in the previous twelve months: 606,000 more people entered the country than left it (this includes asylum seekers, students, family members and those with permission to work here). All of the former holders of this office of state (arguably one of the most challenging roles in government) were united in saying that the stated government target of reducing net migration to under 100,000 per year was unachievable. One spoke of the target as 'vainglorious', another admitted that they never believed in the target even though they had to publicly support it when in office. 'We can't be honest,' said another, 'we want to give the impression that you can do something about it, but it is very, very difficult.' As Kuenssberg pointed out, the fact is that our economy needs immigration, so even as the Home Office tries to slow the rate, the

Treasury is pushing for it to increase. And the drivers behind migration, everything from war, drought, famine and global inequality, are so strong and largely outside the control of politicians, that nothing is going to change it in the foreseeable future.

Not long before the publication of this article, I had been to visit a hotel in Leicestershire which was accommodating asylum seekers. This followed press reports of people protesting outside hotels – one TV report including shocking footage of people chanting, 'Go home. You are not welcome here.' Thankfully, the news reports were balanced by interviews with other residents of the village who understood that 'we are talking about real human beings, with feelings, and hopes and dreams just like us'. However, it was clear that the village was split down the middle. And no doubt part of the resentment was because local people had not been consulted. The hotel had taken out a contract with the Home Office, which would guarantee a near 100% occupancy rate for the hotel, and solve the Home Office's problem of overcrowding in detention centres deemed 'unsafe' and 'dehumanising' by various charities.

Added to this controversy was the announcement that the government wanted to detain and then remove anyone who arrived in the country without legal permission to claim asylum, either to Rwanda or another safe country. The Archbishop of Canterbury used his Easter Sermon to say that the policy posed 'serious ethical questions' and 'would not stand the judgement of God'. One of the former Home Secretaries interviewed by the BBC said, 'it's ridiculous – where are all these thousands of people going to go?'

So, 50 years after the arrival of the Ugandan Asians, there is still little agreement on UK immigration policy! The 2016 Brexit referendum revealed that the UK was split down the middle on the question of our relationship with the 'European project'. So we continue to be confused about our identity as a country, and meanwhile our population continues to rise, and with it our diversity. These are truly bewildering times.

How is the church responding?

I began with a story about Leicester and the current debate on immigration because Leicester has been my home for the last seven years, and the city (and the county to a lesser degree) has been profoundly shaped by immigration. Throughout this book, the 'I' is Martyn, Bishop of Leicester, and, in part, this book offers some of my sabbatical reflections on the last seven years of getting to know this wonderfully diverse city and county. I want to state clearly right at the outset that this is not a 'how to' book when it comes to intercultural church. If you are looking for lots of practical ideas which can be easily slotted into busy church life, this is probably not the book for you (though I do refer to some books which give more practical ideas). Rather it is a book with reflections on my own journey of learning to think and act with a greater degree of cultural sensitivity, and to receive the gift of the other. I hope this will spark ideas and lead to practical changes in the church, but transformation starts in the heart and mind (see Romans 12.2).

For me, Leicester is the latest stage of a cross-cultural journey which started in Indonesia where my parents were missionaries for many years (and my mother's parents and grandparents were missionaries in China), and has included working in such places as Guinea, West Africa and inner-city Sheffield where I was vicar of a multicultural parish for ten years. In Sheffield I experienced for myself just how tough it can be to take an intercultural approach to church and community life. Anyone who sets out on this journey must be prepared for many setbacks, disappointments and challenges. There will often be the temptation to turn back, to take the easier route or give up trying altogether. But while there are less demanding paths, they do not lead to the same vistas or panoramas.

I have been privileged to work with some excellent colleagues over the years, people of many different cultural backgrounds. Among them are: Florence Gildea, my current Social Policy Advisor and co-author of this book (who has worked for two different MPs and also a national charity); Bishop Lusa Nsenga-Ngoy (born in the Democratic Republic of Congo, grew up in Belgium and married to a Dutch woman) who has written the Foreword; Jessie Tang our current Intercultural Ministry Director (born in Bedford, with family roots in South East Asia) who has written an Afterword; and Bishop Saju Muthalaly who has contributed '*Half-time talk – The Gift of Hospitality*'. Bishop Saju has been Bishop of Loughborough (Suffragan Bishop in the Diocese of Leicester) since 2021. He was born and raised in India and came to the UK to do youth work, meeting his English wife here. He brings an understanding of Indian culture which the church in Leicester desperately needed. Bishop Saju, all those mentioned above and many more besides have been inspiring conversation partners as we have explored how the churches of Leicester Diocese can respond to the ever-increasing diversity of our context.

Lusa Nsenga-Ngoy joined our diocesan leadership team in 2017 and was very much responsible for developing the thinking behind our approach to IWCs. He, and our colleague Guli Francis-Dehquani (now Bishop of Chelmsford) argued persuasively for a grant application to the national church which took an intentional approach to both transitioning existing parish churches to become intercultural worshipping communities, and to planting new churches which were intercultural in their core vision and values. This 'mixed ecology' approach – parish churches and fresh expressions/church plants – has been core to our vision for some time and hence it made sense to view both through an intercultural lens.

We knew that this approach was unconventional and potentially hugely demanding. Many have pointed us to research that homogenous church growth (following the principle 'like attracts like' e.g. student congregations) is the way to go. But we remain convinced that a variety of congregational models are needed in order to grow in both numbers and depth of discipleship in our multicultural context. This is the vision given us in the New Testament, and I believe it should be core to the vision of the Church of England. We are a broad church, with local congregations gathered around a bishop in such a way that they are in relationship with other churches of a very different hue (and in relationship with the church nationally and internationally). No local church is complete in and of itself – we need to be in relationship with others. This is the only way that we can embody within the church a vision for wider society – to be a sign, instrument and foretaste of the kingdom of God.[2]

So it has been a steep learning curve for us as a diocese as well as our supporters from the national church. In 2019 Dr Ali Bilgic, a researcher from Loughborough University, carried out extensive interviews with BAME people (a term we have now dropped in favour of Global Majority Heritage (GMH) or UKME) in our six IWCs. I will be drawing extensively on this research and I am grateful to Dr Bilgic for permission to do so.

And the national church response?

This book is intended as a local contribution to the debate on how the church nationally represents the diversity of the communities which we are called to serve. As mentioned above, Leicester is far from unique – there are parts of London, Birmingham, Leeds and Manchester which resemble Leicester – and there will be many more in the years to come. And while our IWCs have been very fruitful in a number of ways, I am not setting out to persuade you that this is the best or only approach. A key part of our learning has been about the importance of context and the need to reflect carefully on what is appropriate for that specific context. So the book is intended as a series of reflections on intercultural gift exchange in the hope that this will generate new perspectives on your own ministry and context.

In 2021, the Church of England articulated its vision and strategy for the 2020s.[3] At the heart of this is a vision for a church which is Jesus Christ centred and Jesus shaped. Then there are three priorities: 'a church of missionary disciples', 'a church where mixed ecology is the norm' and 'a church that is younger and more diverse'.[4] So diversity is explicitly named. But why is this? Is it an implicit endorsement of uncontrolled migration? Is it a turn towards urban ministry where cultural diversity is much more the norm compared with rural ministry? Or are we now saying that diversity itself is a virtue?

The answer to the last of these questions is nuanced, and hence I devote considerable space to it in Chapter 2 '*The Gift of Diversity*'. However, the answer to the first two questions is a resounding 'no' – I am most certainly not arguing for open borders, nor am I arguing that any one context should take priority over others. Rather, I want us to be realistic about the diversity that is already present in all of our communities, and which the church needs to see represented in its own structures. The diversity envisaged by the Church of England is a broad concept. It includes the journey towards parity for women and men in the church. Even though we have women priests and bishops, we are still a long way from true equality (my female colleagues regularly tell me of their continued experiences of sexism in the church). And diversity includes the Living in Love and Faith process which is seeking to ensure people who are lesbian, gay, bisexual, transgender, queer and intersex (LGBTQI+) are welcomed, included and can participate fully in the church (a much broader question than the narrow focus on same-sex marriage). It also includes work to ensure that people with disabilities are similarly included in every aspect of the church's mission and ministry. True diversity means addressing issues of class and socio-economic status (something the Church of England has struggled with much more than some other Christian denominations). And yes, it includes cultural diversity – the focus of this book.

This journey towards cultural diversity is one we have been on for a long time, even though we been moving at a snail's pace. In 2021, the Archbishops' Anti-Racism Taskforce produced a report entitled *From Lament to Action* which described this journey:

In our work as the Taskforce, we have considered 25 [church] reports from the mid-80s onwards with a total of more than 160 recommendations. Since then, the Church of England has considered motion after motion, debate after debate, yet we still find ourselves in the position where – throughout our life as a church – the flourishing of UKME/GMH Anglicans is hard to discern.

However, for all the bleak assessment of the report, the timing was, I believe, truly propitious. It followed not only the mass protests of 2020 after the murder of George Floyd in America, but also a series of other events which truly disrupted the status quo. To name just a few (a selective and UK-focused[5] list):

● **Grenfell Tower, 2017** In the early hours of 14 June 2017, a 24-storey tower block in west London caught fire. Seventy-one people lost their lives – people from many different nationalities, many different backgrounds, but almost all of them, in financial terms, among the least well-off in British society.

- **The 'Windrush scandal', 2017** A Guardian journalist reported the story of 61-year-old Paulette Wilson, who had been living and working in Britain for 50 years when she received a letter informing her that she was an illegal immigrant and was going to be removed to Jamaica, a country she left when she was ten. She was one of an estimated 57,000 long-term citizens who were told they were about to be deported.

- **#MeToo, 2017** Although the hashtag had been used on social media for a number of years, #MeToo exploded into public awareness when a Hollywood actress accused producer Harvey Weinstein of sexual abuse. This led to millions of women around the world sharing their own experiences of harassment and abuse, with particularly strong protests in places such as Iran and Afghanistan.

- **Global climate strike, 2019** Inspired by the teenager Greta Thunberg, over 6 million school children and students walked out of schools and colleges in protest at the lack of action to address the climate crisis, and in particular its disproportionate effect on less economically wealthy nations.

- **Covid-19 pandemic, 2020-23** As of June 2023, it is estimated that 767 million people were infected with nearly 7 million confirmed deaths. Again, the pandemic had a disproportionate effect on poorer nations, but also on GMH people in the UK.

- **Murder of George Floyd/growth of the Black Lives Matter movement, 2020** After an allegation that he had used a counterfeit bank note, George Floyd was arrested and restrained by four police officers, one of whom knelt on his neck for over nine minutes, ignoring his plea 'I can't breathe.' His murder sparked protests around the world, including in the UK where allegations of racism were made against the police and many other institutions.

● **Cost of living crisis, 2021-24**   As well as extreme poverty for many, these years saw economic turmoil following the pandemic and war in Ukraine. At the time of writing, UK inflation rates remain the highest they have been since the 1980s.

Any one of these events could be a generation-defining event. Yet together they have caused the tectonic plates of our world to shift.[6] For the church, this has meant a new awakening to racial and cultural diversity and the challenge both of addressing injustice and ensuring that our churches reflect the communities they serve. Only in the last year or two have we begun to see some real changes: the establishment of a Racial Justice Unit in the national church; the appointment of a number of GMH and UKME bishops; and the Church Commissioners acknowledging the role of slavery within their history and so setting up a £100 million investment fund with a new committee of GMH and UKME people to oversee the use of its income. The Church of England Education Office is also currently in the process of rewriting its *Understanding Christianity* course to ensure that the global church is fully represented in every part of the curriculum. These are all good as far as they go. But I dare to suggest that the real challenge is how we bring about change at the local level, within congregations and communities – hence my offering of intercultural gift exchange as a spur for further reflection.

Why me and why this approach?

Some may wonder how a white, British, middle-aged, multiply-privileged man can have the audacity to write on this subject. We've had centuries of white men pontificating on what the church and society should/must/ought to do. Surely it's time for people like me to sit down, shut up, stop exercising our power and privilege and give space for others to share their wisdom. If this is you, and you have got this far, let me assure you that I have every sympathy with what you are saying, and I almost didn't embark on this project precisely for these reasons. But at the encouragement of various colleagues and friends (of different cultural backgrounds), I offer these reflections as nothing other than a simple contribution to the conversation.

The truth is that I arrived at this intercultural gift exchange approach because I felt sure that, despite my privilege and power, I was denying the gifts that God has given me by not making any contribution. It helps no one to simply dismiss white Western men as having nothing more to contribute. Rather it is a question of *how* we contribute. I hope and pray that I am doing so in an attitude of humility, with an awareness of unhealthy power dynamics and the disparities of this world. For where a position of authority has been conferred, it is incumbent on that person to use that authority wisely and well. So if my contribution, and the platform afforded to me as a bishop, can support the cause of justice and equality for UKME and GMH people, then I will give myself to that work. Challenging racism unequivocally has to involve white people as well as people of colour.

I also want to be clear that this is not about being 'woke' – a term which is now used pejoratively as a way of dismissing those with whom we disagree and with whom we would rather not engage. In fact, I am arguing for a genuine engagement between people of different beliefs and worldviews – something which is increasingly rare in today's society, and something which demands that we stop 'labelling' or 'pigeon-holing' people. So while I want the church to embrace different cultures, this should not be heard as disparaging 'traditional' English culture (however defined). I accept completely that English culture has been profoundly shaped by the Christian faith,[7] and I will be drawing on the long history of reflection on the relationship between the Christian Gospel and culture. I will be arguing for a dialogue between the two, just as there also needs to be a dialogue between people of different cultures. This will be a challenging process – there will be certain things which must be 'let go' and allowed to die, such as our ethnocentrism (believing that our way is the right and only way), and the 'charity begins at home' slogan (which is of course valid, except when it means 'charity stays at home and doesn't extend to anyone who is unlike me').

So for the avoidance of doubt, let me say that I am absolutely not seeking to undermine cherished English institutions and traditions. I love the Church of England for all our foibles and failures, and I count it a privilege to be a custodian of these traditions. I hugely enjoy leading services from *The Book of Common Prayer* in rural churches where there is a sense of countless generations before me having used the same prayers in the same place. I grieve deeply over the falling numbers attending many of our churches and long for a renewal of faith across our nation. And yet I agree with those who have observed that renewal usually comes from the edges, rather than the centre.

I also agree with those who have pointed out that questions of national identity and national pride are extremely important. Nigel Biggar in his recent work *Colonialism: A Moral Reckoning* is right to say that our self-understanding and our confidence in our values and our role within the world today has been significantly affected by those who paint our history of colonialism as entirely evil. But, in my opinion, he is wrong to argue (and this is his central argument) that this can be corrected by relativising the evils of British colonialism, suggesting that they were nothing compared to the violence of other empires, and were outweighed by the good done by our ancestors.[8] In my view, it is possible to take pride in who we are today and our contribution to the community of nations, while also acknowledging the terrible wrongs done by our ancestors (wrongs we will go on repeating unless we are prepared to be honest with ourselves and think critically).

On the other side of this debate, I am also aware that some may see the arguments of this book around interculturalism as an attempt to reconcile that which cannot be reconciled. When such injustice has been done to people of colour – from the transatlantic slave trade, to a market system rigged against the poor in Africa, Asia and South America, to ongoing institutional racism in the Church of England[9] – surely church leaders must side with those who are oppressed rather than seeking a compromise between the oppressors and those they continue to abuse. I suspect this would be the view of James Cone, author of *A Black Theology of Liberation* (among many other books) who died in 2008. Reading his books, there is a palpable sense of his anger at injustice, and a feeling that no white person, however well-meaning, can fully understand the pain. However, I want to be clear that my approach is a separate yet linked task to that of challenging racism and injustice. We absolutely need to do the latter (and I write as a member of the Committee for Minority Ethnic Anglican Concerns – the Church of England committee tasked with working alongside the Racial Justice Unit to challenge racism and prejudice), yet we also need to find a way forward which includes everyone. So I sincerely hope what I am offering is not a simplistic appeal to 'move on' as if the pain of centuries can just be brushed aside, but rather an honest attempt to lament, to repent and to offer a positive, hopeful vision for the future.

My sincere hope is that this book will help to develop a wider conversation in our churches and communities. I hope this is a book which church leaders will feel happy recommending to people in their churches. I hope it will inspire discussions in small groups. Everyone has something to contribute to this conversation – including those who trace their English ancestry back to the Domesday Book and those whose ancestry lies in the great migrations out of India or China, those who have been refugees, whether from Nazi Germany or from Iran, and those who have 'hybrid' identities with mixed ancestors and multiple cultures. It includes those who can't read or write, those whose poor mental health means they think they have nothing to contribute, those who are hidden to wider society in a care home or prison or bedsit, those who don't speak English, and those who are fearful that their views and opinions are no longer politically correct and therefore they will be pilloried for expressing them. We (our society) need the gifts of all these people. We all have something to give and something to receive, and I hope this book will help advance a conversation about *how* we give and receive. In continuing this conversation, and learning the posture and skills of intercultural gift exchange, I believe we will discover something more of God's kingdom and find ourselves captivated by the beauty of God, the Holy Trinity – the diverse yet unified creator, redeemer and sustainer of all life.

Towards intercultural gift exchange

Intercultural gift exchange is the thread running through this text. In the next chapter, I will start with the complex issue of diversity. While arguing that diversity can be received as a gift, I also acknowledge that gifts come with a complex mix of expectations, some unhelpful. But it is my hope that the church in general will embrace diversity to a much greater extent than has been the case up until now. And because this book is focusing on the issue of cultural diversity (there are many other good books on other forms of diversity), I will go on to explore a postmodern understanding of culture (again with many layers of complexity) and link this to interculturalism as the deliberate act of reflecting on how cultures interact for good and ill. I will give an example of a church in Leicester which has made a surprising journey in this direction, and also reflect on the well-known story of Peter and Cornelius in Acts 10 and 11 and its dynamic of the dominant culture becoming the minority and vice versa.

Chapter 3 introduces the much misunderstood field of gift exchange. Gifts come in surprising shapes and sizes. And I will start with the questions of whether we can see ourselves as a gift to others, as well as seeing *the other* as a gift to us. This is more challenging than it may sound, particularly in the context of racism and our history of colonialism. It is hard for someone to view themselves as a gift if they have long been told they are 'subhuman' or if their own history and culture has been re-written by colonizers.

There is a long history of debate on the subject of gift exchange going back to Aristotle and Cicero. As far as we are aware, most ancient societies were based on a form of gift exchange. And while this lapsed in Europe with the rise of rationalism and capitalism, it was 're-discovered' by anthropologists such as Marcel Mauss. But this long history has much to teach us on the place of power and privilege within gift exchange. So there is an urgent need to recapture what 'healthy' gift exchange entails. My proposal is threefold – generous giving, radical receptivity and transformative thanksgiving. On this last point, I will argue that it is only when God is included in the 'circle of gifts' that we can overcome the negative expectations.

My colleague Bishop Saju Muthalaly then offers a 'Half-time talk' (to use a football or rugby metaphor – Leicester is a sporting city, after all!). Saju spent the first twenty years of his life in India and here he sets out his understanding of hospitality and what it means to be both guest and host. This is a form of intercultural gift exchange and provides an excellent worked example of what this book is advocating.

In Chapter 4, I move to models of intercultural theology, another burgeoning field in universities and colleges around the world. But the term encompasses very different approaches, from courses which focus on Christian mission and the translation of the gospel into different cultures, to those which explore the maturation of majority world theologies and their challenge to the dominant Western approach. Still others go well beyond Christianity and merge into a study of world religions. I will argue that an intercultural gift exchange model has much to offer across this spectrum (including current approaches to interfaith work and ecumenical ministry e.g. receptive ecumenism). However, the essential point is that the Western church must learn to de-centre itself and counter 'white normativity' i.e. stop thinking that our way of doing things is the only way and the right way! And since Anglicanism has traditionally expressed its theology in liturgy, I will explore what intercultural theology and gift exchange might look like in terms of our liturgy.

Finally, I will return to the wider social and political realm. If the church embarks on this intercultural journey, what does this mean for our presence in a multicultural world? The implications are potentially huge, and this chapter will do no more than scratch the surface in exploring how intercultural gift exchange might be applied at a macro level by government. My argument is that government can only do this in a very particular way – by putting in place a framework which allows for the growth of intercultural friendships and cultural competency. These are the basic building blocks for a cohesive society. Yet I will also give what I hope is an honest account of how things have not always gone well in my own city of Leicester – we have much to learn from our mistakes as well as from our creativity and innovation.

Jessie Tang, our Intercultural Ministry Director then offers an afterword about our future hopes for developing this work in Leicester. Jessie is an ethnomusicologist who has challenged us to think about different approaches to music and worship which help everyone to find their place within our churches. She leads a diverse team who are growing the participation and engagement of GMH people in every area of the life of the diocese.

I want to reiterate that this book is intended as no more than an offering to a bring-and-share meal. We are all invited to the table to eat. Even more than this, we are all invited to the kitchen to share in the cooking. I am not seeking to be the master chef. History, and current realities, would suggest that I am the last person who should take on that role. But, what I have, I offer. I do so with a prayer that you find it nourishing and tasty. I hope and pray that there will be many other offerings in the years to come.

2. The Gift of Diversity

In this chapter, I'll be exploring:

● diversity as both good and complex;

● current understandings of culture and interculturalism;

● one church's journey towards interculturalism;

● the call to be converted to God and the other.

Omar, the young, Muslim café-owner, greets me warmly. I'm one of his regulars. He knows my order before I say it. He asks me about my plans for the day. 'Still working on the book – hoping your coffee will help overcome my writer's block,' I joke. 'Well, make sure you tell them about Narborough Road,' he entreats me, 'it's the world in a street.'

Narborough Road is a mile-long stretch of shops and bars, cafés and restaurants in Leicester's West End. Recent research revealed that the owners of these enterprises hail from 22 different countries around the world.[10] The lead researcher Dr Suzanne Hall commented:

What we found in Narborough Road was staggering, really. It is the world in microcosm; all these people, from all these different places, different cultures, living cheek by jowl, working with each other and living in harmony. And it works, too.

On a practical level, this means that the entrepreneurial store owners trade their skills with each other as a kind of parallel currency. Dr Hall explains,

> There is a Canadian couple who run a book shop on Narborough
> Road. They're what's known as 'anchor immigrants'. They've
> been there a long time. Because their English is good and they
> know about forms and bureaucracy, they help the other traders.
> In return, they get a free haircut, or lunch at a restaurant, on the
> house. They trade their services with each other as favours...
> and they learn from each other, too. That's interesting. In austere
> times, people are not just investing money, they invest hope and
> care. We should not ignore the role migrants play in places like
> this. They don't just live here. They invest here. They make [these
> communities] work.[11]

The story of streets like this is the story of our times. It is a story of
immigration, change and diversity. It's the story of globalization and
its impact on local communities. It's one part of the story of colonialism
and its legacy. And it's an example of intercultural gift exchange –
people of different cultures giving and receiving gifts in a way that
creates community.

For some this is a fascinating mix of cultures, a near utopia which
embodies humanity's diversity and our ability to live with difference –
a perfect place for a piece of research! The chatter of multiple
languages, the aroma of exotic spicy foods, the spectacle of contrasting
clothing, some colourful and reminiscent of holidays in hot climates,
others mysterious in their expression of different values.

And yet, for many who live in these communities, the story is rather
different. Yes, those who live on or around Narborough Road take pride
in their community, and rightly so. But I suspect that for many of them,
the diversity is less a fascination and more a fact of life and a daily
reminder of the injustices of past, present and anticipated future. Their

journey to this country may have been traumatic. Their welcome in this country may have been at best lukewarm, at worst a 'hostile environment' (to quote a former Home Secretary). And the necessity of navigating an unfamiliar bureaucracy in a second or third language will probably have been exhausting and at times soul-destroying. Then there may have been the expectations of sending money and gifts back to their home country to support elderly parents or young siblings. Gift exchange can be a heavy burden, and such obligations truly matter in the majority of cultures around the world.

In addition, there are the people who don't live in these communities but who drive through them – usually with car doors locked – and look on with a sense of bewilderment. Why do people want to come to this country when it is clear to everyone that the streets are not paved with gold? And why can't the government do more to stop them and slow the pace of change? What has happened to 'the country of long shadows on county grounds, warm beer, invincible green suburbs, dog lovers and pools fillers and – as George Orwell said – "old maids bicycling to Holy Communion through the morning mist"' (to quote former Prime Minister John Major)?

In my introduction, I stated that cultural diversity is here to stay. And I want to argue that this is a good thing – diversity can be seen as a gift. But as the different perceptions of Narborough Road reveal, people have very different views on this. So, let me start with the positives before then exploring some of the complexities.

Diversity is good

Theologically, diversity is a rich concept. It is undoubtedly a 'good' of creation – Genesis 1 tells us that God saw creation in all its diversity and declared it good. And God instituted the Sabbath as time to rest and enjoy the goodness and diversity of creation. However, after the fall, the diversity of humanity became the source of competition, fear, hatred and violence. And so the story of the Tower of Babel (Genesis 11) marks both the climax of diversity (all the nations had different languages as described in Genesis 10), yet also speaks of an attempt to impose unity by force. Jonathan Sacks[12] viewed this as the first story of colonialism, written no doubt with the Babylonian empire in view – a colonial power seeking to assimilate diverse people groups into one culture and nation. Yet God 'came down to see the city and tower, which mortals had built' (and which they comically thought was so big) and scatters them, liberating the peoples from this empire and its imperialism. So Babel is not a story of scattering (as often suggested) but rather the first story of liberation from captivity (a theme which is central to much of the Old Testament).

This approach to Genesis 11 also suggests a rather different approach to the most common interpretation of Acts 2 and the account of Pentecost. The Holy Spirit appears as tongues of fire on the heads of the disciples and 'they began to speak in other languages as the Spirit gave them ability.' The onlookers are amazed as they hear their own language being spoken by these uneducated Galileans. Others think they are drunk. So, this story is sometimes interpreted as God reversing the scattering of Babel and overcoming diversity. Yet as Joel Edwards points out in his Foreword to *Intercultural Preaching*,[13] 'This moment of the church's inception was the sanctification of difference ... a church birthed in diversity. It was God's way of saying, "I talk your language."' So, diversity need no longer be the cause of fear, hatred and violence. Pentecost stands as a sign of God's continuing work of liberation from colonising forces. The church is founded on the principle that diversity is good and can be celebrated, because the same Spirit is at work in all of us.

Professor Lamin Sanneh, a Gambian theologian and historian, who worked for many years at Yale University, devoted his life to studying both Christianity and Islam. He came to the extraordinary conclusion that the difference between the two can be summed up in one word: 'translatability'.

Unlike Islam, Christianity has no revealed language. The Gospels are a translation of the teaching and preaching of Jesus. Both religions are missionary, but Islam does mission by promoting an untranslated Qur'an, valid only in the original Arabic, whereas Christianity, by contrast, does mission entirely by translation. Christianity spawns variety and diversity because it is invested in translation, which is dependent on interpretation.[14]

The incarnation is the supreme example of this – 'the Word became flesh' (John 1.14). And if the incarnation is both a unique event (or person – Jesus Christ), and a principle for Christian mission (translation – or, as Sam Wells puts it, 'being with' people in all their diversity[15]), it follows that every church in every culture will be different. God speaks the local language, and God's compassion and love must be 'translated' into each culture and context. And in contexts where multiple cultures interact, this means multiple languages and the different thought-forms that accompany language (notwithstanding the need to have a common language to enable communication – in the context of England, this has to be English).

The rest of the New Testament tells us that we have nothing to fear by this plurality of thought-forms, even though the writers are honest about the challenges. Diversity is not crushed by the coming of the Spirit. Rather, the colours become more vivid, the perspective deepens and we see more of the fullness of life which Jesus offers our world. This is expressed in the church, described in the New Testament as 'the body of Christ'. Matthew Salisbury explains:

The use of a metaphor involving parts of the body is long attested in pre-Christian texts. But Paul is distinct in saying that *God is the cause* of the diversity of the members and their particular relationships to one another, and also to say that they are all/each to use their gifts for the common good, rather than subordinating some of them 'for the good of the whole'.

In the Eucharist, the epitome of Christian community action (writes John Zizioulas), 'otherness of a natural or social kind can be transcended'. In fact, 'otherness is inconceivable apart from relationship' – the communion modelled by the persons of the Trinity 'does not threaten otherness; it generates it' ... Ralph McMichael shows that it is through the body of Christ gathered 'that we are able to see the face of Christ in others; knowledge of the one Christ in the variety of members of his Body'. The location of the Eucharist 'cannot be determined by geography, culture, institutions, language.'[16]

To add to this, the Bible is unambiguous in offering a vision of heaven with people from the East and West, North and South. And Revelation 7.9 is the culmination of this, the rallying cry for all those who believe in intercultural church: 'After this I looked, and there was a great multitude that no one could count, from every nation, from all tribes and peoples and languages, standing before the throne and before the Lamb, robed in white, with palm branches in their hands.'

Diversity is complex – the need for humility

Having said all this, there is a lively debate about whether diversity can be seen as a theological virtue. Classically, it hasn't been viewed as such – the theological virtues, understood as a grace of God disposing us to act in a morally good way, are faith, hope and charity/love (1 Corinthians 13), and the cardinal virtues described by Plato are prudence, justice, fortitude and temperance. Yet diversity can be shown to relate to each of these virtues, sometimes in a very obvious way such as loving our neighbour as ourselves, however different they may be to us. Sometimes the relationship is more subtle, as in the need for prudence or wisdom when wrestling with moral diversity. Can we accept all behaviours or are there limits to diversity in this realm? Perhaps the furthest we can go is to say that diversity can be a good training ground for the virtues while not itself being a virtue.

This also applies to the way we do theology (see Chapter 4). The Bible has to be read in community otherwise our own biases will shape our interpretation (or to put it another way, our fallenness indicates the necessity for humility when seeking to understand and apply scripture). Yet this is bound to be deeply challenging, and raises profound questions about our ways of 'knowing' and our understanding of truth. Cultures have very different understandings of knowledge and truth,[17] and we can easily fall into the trap of assuming that Western ways of knowing must be universal.[18] For those of us who have studied theology at Western institutions, it is hard to appreciate just how much we have been shaped by Greek philosophy, medieval scholasticism, Reformation theology (or the reaction to it) or the Caroline Divines and the Oxford Movement. Often it is not until we encounter someone who has been shaped by different cultural and theological streams that we start to realize the need for humility with regard to our own cultural context.

As an example of this, consider the process we go through when we visit another country. We start by noticing all that is different – the language, the weather, the way people drive, the customs of hospitality. However, after a few days, the novelty starts to wear off and we find ourselves discombobulated and then frustrated. Even the most basic of tasks can be hard work. Usually, it is only if we stay beyond a few weeks that we eventually get to the point where we start to be able to question why things are done differently in this country. What are the values that underlie particular behaviours? For example, the different understanding of time in some parts of Africa – it took me a little while to realize that it was far more important to stop, greet a friend and chat with them on the road, than it was to be on time for a meeting! And eventually, when we have overcome our irritation and started to get familiar with a new way of doing things, we reach a point where we start to question why things are done in a certain way in our home country. Why is it so important to be on time for a meeting in the UK? What does this say about the value we place on relationships? Hence the need to cultivate cultural humility which recognizes the good in all cultures and does not seek the replacement of one culture by another.

However, arguing for cultural humility is not the same as accepting relativism i.e. I am not saying that nothing can be criticized in another culture. Rather, as Lesslie Newbigin[19] has argued, even though there is no neutral place from which to evaluate different cultures (the mistake of modernism), nevertheless it is our embeddedness in a particular culture which allows us to enter into a healthy dialogue with other cultures – as long as we are prepared to be humble and accept others' critique of our culture.

Consider for a moment the parallels between interfaith work and Christian ecumenical work (I explore this in more detail in Chapter 4). Interfaith dialogue and partnership working is a core part of my work in Leicester and I hugely enjoy it, even though at times it can be deeply challenging. When asked why I enjoy it, my response is usually along the lines that engaging with people of other faiths helps me go deeper in my own faith. I still hold to the uniqueness of Christ, and I don't gloss over the differences in our beliefs, but I am led to critically assess why I believe and do certain things.

As an example, I was challenged recently by a Jewish friend about my interpretation of the parable of the Good Samaritan. She found the story deeply offensive in its criticism of the priest and Levite and the commendation of the Samaritan. 'Have you stopped to think what this feels like for a British Jew?' she asked me. I had to admit that I had not, and so I looked again at the passage. It is of course a response to the question 'Who is my neighbour?' and hence a worked example of what it means to love your neighbour as yourself. What this looks like in twenty-first century Britain will be quite different from first century Palestine. So I now preach on the passage with much greater sensitivity as well as more focus on the core message. And thankfully our friendship survived this cultural insensitivity on my part!

A different example is that of the many new Pentecostal churches springing up in Leicester (and around the country). These churches are often quite culturally specific with congregations drawn from a particular diaspora community from Africa or Asia. In these churches, there is a strong focus on prayer for healing and a theology of Christ's victory over the devil and what this means in the reality of daily life. As the style of worship may be very different to that of many Anglican churches, we can sometimes fail to see the gifts they offer. Interviews with Black majority church leaders in Leicester suggest that many find their relationships with White majority churches very difficult. Sometimes this is because the interactions are transactional rather than relational – for example, if the Black majority church wants to rent a church building and is presented with a contract and a list of demands for different policies. There is little relationship in a legal document. And when there is a relationship, the assumption is still that they (the Black majority church) need to learn how we (the White majority church) do things. In this way, host churches or societies show little understanding for just how hard it is to adapt to a new culture, and just how scary it can be when your immigration status is constantly being questioned. It is really no wonder that many immigrants choose to attend churches with others of their own culture. This can be one of the only safe spaces for them. Hence the challenge of this book – how can Anglican churches become a safe space for people of all backgrounds?

So, in different ways, the diversity of other faith groups and other Christian groups offer gifts to the Church of England. Yet in both cases the key to receiving these gifts is cultural humility and wisdom. Are we confident enough in our core beliefs that we are not scared of encountering difference and examining why we believe the things we do? And are we humble enough to accept that our way of doing things is not the only way – are we open to learn from the other? 'Confident humility' or 'humble confidence' is a key theme throughout this book.

Diversity is complex – the need for wisdom

The term 'diversity' covers a wide range of characteristics. The nine 'protected characteristics' in UK law are age, disability, gender reassignment, marriage and civil partnership, pregnancy and maternity, race, religion or belief, sex and sexual orientation. I have already spoken about 'cultural diversity' as the focus of this book, yet it is important to acknowledge the intersectionality of the different protected characteristics. This probably requires a book of its own but it is my own belief that there are certain unique elements to each of the protected characteristics, while there are also commonalities and intersections. So while I am focusing on cultural diversity (which incidentally is different to nationality, language spoken or colour of skin), I hope that readers will also have an eye to other protected characteristics and the implications of my arguments for these.

However, I'm not convinced that the current trend for promoting equality, diversity and inclusion always helps. All organisations in the West today (including churches) are expected to have an EDI statement which outlines their commitment to these values and how they practice them. This is certainly a step forward from the era when such things were simply not discussed. Yet when reading these statements, it often feels that the understanding of diversity is quite thin i.e. lacking an exploration of the complexities. There is an implicit assumption that prescribing respect for diversity in law (with sanctions taken against anyone who does not have due regard to these values) is the best way of achieving the intended outcome. Law has its place, but if what we really want is for everyone to 'do unto others as you would have them do unto you' then arguably, more attention should be given to how we create an environment for growth in the virtues, rather than assuming law alone can hammer home the changes.

Similarly, there is much talk in some circles of the 'diversity advantage': on boards and committees it has been shown that greater diversity leads to better discussions (with a wider range of views) and hence better decision-making. Again there is truth to this, but there is also a live debate about whether this should be made a requirement or whether it should grow naturally out of wider approaches to inclusion and engagement. Simply having one woman or one person of colour on an otherwise all white, male board does not constitute diversity. Research has shown that unless there are several representatives of different groups on a board it is unlikely that different views will be expressed, listened to and allowed to shape the decision-making.

The title of this chapter, '*The Gift of Diversity*', is not intended therefore as a simplistic endorsement of a current trend in Western society. As we will see when we come to consider gift exchange in the next chapter, gifts can also carry negative expectations as well as being a positive contribution. However, I am arguing in this chapter that the current reality of a diversity of cultures in our cities and towns is a gift which should be received as such, even if at times this is complex.

Cultural diversity – where are we now?

Cultural diversity has its roots in the fact that we are a nation of immigrants. If we go back far enough, all our family histories will include stories of immigration – whether Norman, Viking, Celtic or Asian, African, Latin American. Our family histories will probably also include stories of emigration – various members of my wider family emigrated to the USA and I discovered recently one who was among the first convicts deported to Australia! We are all 'cultural hybrids' – not just in terms of our ancestry, but also in terms of where and when we were born, where we have lived and with whom we've mixed. I imagine that most of us rebelled against our parents' culture at some point in our youth and hence developed a hybrid culture between that of our parents and that of our peers!

For diaspora communities, this last point takes on particular significance. As one African parent commented to me recently, 'Most African diaspora children see themselves in a colonial relationship with their parents – they believe they have been colonized by their parents' culture.' This refers to the very complex journey for second and third generation immigrants of exploring their identity. In the home, there may be a very strong African culture, including language, food, customs and traditions, but when the children go to school and they must fit in with a very English culture. There can be a sense in which they feel that they don't belong to either. And parents can be very sensitive about their children 'rejecting' their cultural roots.

This confusion over identity is now shown clearly in census figures with the number of people identifying in 2021 as 'any other ethnic background' going up considerably i.e. people who do not see themselves as fitting into the neat categories on the census form. And while cultural diversity and racial diversity are not the same thing, they are clearly closely related.

A comparison of the census figures in 2001 and 2021 show that racial diversity has increased significantly in the last 20 years:

- the percentage of people in the White British ethnic group went down from 87.5% to 74.4%;

- the percentage of people in the Other White ethnic group showed the biggest percentage point increase, from 2.6% to 6.2% – this group includes people born in Poland, the second largest group of residents born outside the UK (743,100) behind people born in India (920,400);

- the proportion of people who identify as Asian more than doubled – with this increase being shared across each of the sub-categories;

- the proportion of people who identify as Mixed ethnicity has more than doubled, with a similar level of increase across all the sub-categories;

- the proportion of people who identify as Black has nearly doubled, with this increase concentrated in the Black African ethnic group, which has nearly tripled.

In my own local context of Leicester, the 2021 census revealed that 40.9% of Leicester's population are White, 43.4% Asian or Asian British, 7.8% Black or Black British and 3.8% Mixed or multiple heritage. So somewhere between 2012 and 2015, the white population of Leicester became a minority.

Population projections are necessarily based upon assumptions about the future behaviour of three demographic drivers: fertility, mortality and migration – with fertility and migration being interrelated and very difficult to predict. Immigrants typically have a younger age profile than the general population (73% of non-UK born residents in the 2021 census were under the age of 30, and 91% were under 44). Therefore, they contribute more to the birth rate and less to the mortality rate. The white British share of the population is, therefore, likely to continue to fall in coming decades, given the lower average age and higher birth rate of minority populations combined with a continued higher level of immigration.

Despite the 'smoothing' effect of globalization, as racial diversity increases so does cultural diversity – becoming more complex as different cultures and attitudes interact. It is this interaction between different cultures that interculturalism seeks to explore.

Culture and interculturalism

It has been said[20] that every human person is in certain respects:

1. like all others
2. like some others
3. like no other.

The first assertion refers to the characteristics that all human persons have in common. The third points to the uniqueness of each individual. But the second recognizes that we are shaped and influenced by the community/communities within which we are socialized. This is the matrix of values, beliefs, customs and basic life assumptions which we call culture.

Anthony Gittens, Professor Emeritus of Theology and Culture at the Catholic Theological Union in Chicago has written widely on interculturalism (or interculturality as he refers to it). In his book *Living Mission Interculturally*,[21] he explores the term 'culture' in considerable detail, noting that it is fluid and hard to pin down:

There are several hundred definitions of this shape-changing term, and ... all of them can be classified under one of four broad categories: classicist, evolutionary, modern, and postmodern. Briefly, classicist definitions identify culture in the singular: some (a few, privileged) people or societies have it; others do not, or only in an attenuated form. An evolutionary perspective, by contrast, classifies cultures, contemporary and historical, somewhere on an ascending scale, that is topped by the European culture (or civilisation), which, not surprisingly, happens to be that of the very people who created the definition in the first place.

By the late nineteenth century, however, people were beginning to identify a great plurality of cultures, and using the word to describe the constellation of characteristics that defined or described particular social groups (usually a tribe, caste, or nation). Whereas *classicist* definitions tended to see culture as fixed and frozen, *modern* definitions tended to compare cultures to clocks or organisms: each part has a specific function contributing to the whole... *Postmodern* definitions now tend to romanticise culture much less, to minimise the scientific nature of anthropology itself in favour of a more 'interpretive' approach to cultural manifestations, and to view cultures not as discrete or static entities, but as constantly 'contested' (a helpful notion, this) by their members, who struggle to reinvent themselves, to make new choices, or simply to survive.

This notion of cultures as constantly changing and contested is a helpful starting point for thinking about interculturalism. It may be that I have already slipped into speaking of cultures in a rather romantic way (as if everything different or 'exotic' is good). But I am all too aware from my work that the question of culture in our country and in the Church of England is highly contested (often with unpleasant arguments on social media). However, in one sense there is nothing new about this – Alasdair MacIntyre in *After Virtue* (1988) described 'tradition' as a people in conversation with each other, over time, about who they are, how they live and how they relate to others. A tradition dies when it ceases to be an ongoing debate about what it means to live within that tradition. So, in this view, the current debate in society and church is healthy and a sign of the vitality of our traditions. Yet here I go again, romanticizing something which in theory is good, yet in practice is often expressed in deeply unhealthy ways!

Homi K. Bhabha,[22] one of the founding fathers of postcolonialism (a growing field of studies about how people have responded to colonialism) is widely associated with coining the term 'hybridity' to describe the way in which all cultures have been shaped by their interaction with other cultures. He is clear that 'all cultures are hybrid cultures' meaning there is a continual process of hybridization as people interact. In reality Bhabha was simply borrowing a term widely used in other fields (from biology to linguistics to racial theory) but he employed it within a colonizer/colonized context in order to stress the 'contradictory and ambivalent' space in which cultures mix/borrow/reject/transform one another. Key to understanding this is the recognition of the power differences involved.[23]

Interculturalism then, is the process of reflection on the interaction of cultures with the intention of ensuring that all people are equally valued, all are able to contribute their unique gifts, and receive the gifts of others. This is essential if we are to address power differentials. When people of different cultures interact, there is always a power differential, whether acknowledged or not. Sometimes this is very stark, as with empire building (imposing one culture over another). Sometimes it is subtle and related to 'soft power' e.g. different cultural understandings of relationships, status, deference and submissiveness. Without an awareness of such cultural issues, we are left stumbling in the dark – bumping into each other, often causing hurt even when we are well-intentioned.

There is an interesting political question here (to which we will return): should government (local or national) intervene in this natural process of different cultures influencing one another, or should individuals and communities be left to work it out for themselves? My own belief is that the power dynamics demand that government is involved in this process, but it is a limited role which needs careful definition (see Chapter 5). And citizens must also be equipped to reflect on their everyday encounters with people of different cultures and learn the skills of interculturalism. This is similar to all we have been learning about safeguarding, which at its heart is about recognizing power differentials and knowing how to protect the most vulnerable. Just as we need government to enact and enforce laws which seek to prevent harm, so too we need citizens who are committed and equipped to safeguard every individual. The same applies to issues of culture – there has to be a partnership across all levels of society in order to ensure the flourishing of people of all cultures.

The approach of interculturalism then, is in stark contrast to assimilation which seeks to absorb differences as quickly as possible into one dominant culture and to create a homogenous group of people. An example of this is the 'melting pot' approach which for some time was much vaunted in the USA. According to this narrative, as people arrived in the USA from all over the world, a new American culture was created with ingredients from their respective cultures. Much as this was an attractive vision for many, it took little account of racism. For years, indigenous people and those of colour were forced to assimilate into the dominant American culture. In Europe too the melting pot turned out to be another example of eurocentrism, with power and privilege kept in the hands of those with the 'right' ancestry.[24]

Interculturalism is also a very different approach to multiculturalism which celebrates the coexistence of numerous cultures, none of which take precedence or have higher value. On the plus side, this has enabled minority cultures to be maintained and not be swallowed up or assimilated by the majority culture. But it also falls short with respect to the complexities of cultures and the interaction between them. People draw from multiple cultures and traditions and may combine multiple identities. Their sense of identity can be influenced by attributes such as age, gender, disability, sexuality, class and how they intersect with ethnicity, culture, language and faith. Multiculturalism often means categorising people into fixed one-dimensional boxes. This understanding of groups perpetuates an 'us/them' paradigm, and can lead to the marginalization of migrant cultures, perpetuating poverty and exclusion through ghettoization.

Interculturalism, then, is a way of drawing on the gift of diversity while also paying attention to the complex dynamics involved when cultures meet one another. It is not offering an easy solution to the problems of power, privilege, prejudice and history – these are realities which won't simply disappear. But it does draw our attention to them, warning us to beware, think carefully and be open to change.

Therefore no one is immune from this process of hybridization – except hermits isolated from other humans! For white British people like me, the process of interculturalism is deeply challenging because it involves 'de-centring' our own culture and entering into a humble yet confident engagement with people of other cultures, with an openness to being changed by the encounter.

For people of other cultures in the UK this process of interculturalism is deeply challenging because it is so personal and raises profound questions of identity. As already mentioned, 'hybridity' can cause a painful sense of not really belonging anywhere, as people have to constantly construct and reconstruct their own identity in dialogue with other cultures. And having to do this in a context where others don't understand the issues can be lonely and isolating. This is why interculturalism is such an urgent calling for the whole church.

Benedictine spirituality has something profound to offer here. For all that Benedictine monasteries are enclosed, stable communities (monks stay for most of their lives and they have little direct contact with the outside world), they believe that 'these are the people that God has given me, in order that I may learn how to love'. Anyone who has an idealized view of the gifts of community can quickly become disillusioned on realizing it means learning to live with people who may annoy, frustrate and challenge in equal measure. The aim of these communities is not just to tolerate one another's foibles and idiosyncrasies, but rather to learn to love the whole person. In a sense, marriage, family life and close friendships operate in a similar way (which is why they are so hard, and we may find ourselves wanting to run away). And church communities too are intended to be a space where our character is formed and the virtues grow within us. Even as we struggle in learning to love the other, the Eucharist draws us back, again and again, to God's forgiveness, acceptance and commissioning of us as baptized disciples.

This is why I am so enthusiastic about a vision for intercultural church. For churches can be a place where people who are very different come together, see one another as a gift from God and learn how to love. Perhaps I am being naive and idealistic, but I have glimpsed the reality of this and I will dare to go on believing that this is our calling.

All Saints Church, Belgrave and the journey towards interculturalism

Sunny George and his family have been an extraordinary blessing to me in my ministry in Leicester. Sunny is of Indian heritage and he is now ordained and overseeing the congregation of All Saints in Belgrave – the area of Leicester sometimes referred to as 'Little India'. This congregation reveals something of the complex diversity of Leicester. Anyone who knows the subcontinent of India will grasp how extraordinary it is that there are significant numbers of people of Indian heritage and of Pakistani heritage in one congregation. Indeed, Sunny has mentored a woman of Pakistani heritage who got involved in ministry in the church, became a Reader and was then ordained. She is currently serving her curacy elsewhere in the diocese and has been a great blessing to many.

The history of the congregation is fascinating. It began as the United Asian Christian Fellowship – an independent church with the vision of being an intercultural church for people from the Asian subcontinent. Sunny was appointed pastor and the church met in various locations around the city. They heard that an Anglican Church in Belgrave was due to close and approached the diocese. It is worth saying that this densely populated parish of over 40,000 people is one of the largest in the Church of England. Seventy years ago, it was served by six churches and a team of clergy. As the demographics of the area changed, so the churches shrank and four of the six churches closed. The fifth was due to close when Sunny approached my predecessor and he, with typical foresight, suggested that instead of buying or renting the building, they consider joining the Church of England. So began a long journey of exploring the theology, theory and practice of being an intercultural church within the predominantly white Church of England.

Sunny has been exceptionally gracious in this process. Expectation after expectation has been laid upon him and his congregation, from ordination training and curacy, to safeguarding, finance, charity law, the appointment of a church council and church officers, annual meetings, faculty regulations, liturgy, baptism and confirmation practices, funerals and weddings, deanery and diocesan synods… the list goes on and on. I have found myself apologizing again and again to Sunny because the process has essentially been one of assimilation. We started by saying 'It's so good that you want to be part of the Church of England', and then we said, 'and here's a list of things you will need to change in order to become like us.'

Now please don't misread this. I am certainly not saying that it is unreasonable to expect a new congregation to have to learn about good safeguarding practice and good financial management and accountability. Such things are essential for any congregation in any part of the world. There are also some things which are core to the identity of the Church of England and therefore non-negotiable – though exactly what should be included in this list is highly contentious. But I suspect that a lot of what we have demanded of Sunny and All Saints are parts of 'our' culture (by which I mean English culture and the Church of England sub-culture) which are less to do with our core identity and more to do with our 'cultural superiority' i.e. our assumption that we know best how to do these things. Recognition of the gifts that Sunny and his congregation bring to the Diocese of Leicester and the Church of England has often been lacking in this process.

The church building is located on a busy junction immediately opposite the largest Hindu temple in Leicester. When I visited recently, there was bunting across the large open space at the back of the church, flower arrangements on the pillars, bright green satin altar cloths, and a cart that had been used for a sweet stall at a recent party. There is a visual vibrancy and eclectic aesthetic to the church which suggests a living faith and active community. And there are immediate symbols of South Asian culture. The architecture of the building and its internal layout is not imposing, and doesn't imply any hierarchies or predefined ways of using the space.

In response to local food poverty the church runs a 'food pantry' – a development of food banks where members pay a small weekly fee to choose a certain number of food items and receive opportunities to train or volunteer. And after every service the congregation has a meal together – several members work in restaurants and takeaways in the city, so the church food is top quality!

Hospitality is absolutely central to their approach to mission. Indeed, Sunny regularly quotes an Indian proverb, 'A guest is like a god.' He and his wife have clearly been key to setting this culture of hospitality and many people have spoken of their warmth and practical help. Sunny commented recently that for him, 'hospitality takes precedence over rules' – an interesting reflection on the experience of joining the Church of England.

A review of All Saints' journey, conducted by the Archdeacon of Leicester (who has lived most of his life in Leicester and is committed to intercultural learning) highlighted both the huge strengths of All Saints and its impact within the local community, while also pointing to failings within diocesan support structures. Many of us (including me) simply didn't understand South Asian cultures and were too swift to impose English norms with little reflection. And perhaps we assumed that the church would proactively ask for help if they got into difficulty, without understanding different cultural attitudes to seeking support. It's been a steep learning curve for us all, now greatly helped by the IWC programme.

This is just one example of a journey towards interculturalism but it highlights some of the challenges. All Saints has become a safe space for people of many different cultures who struggle to find places they can call 'home' and people they can call 'family' (a word which comes up a lot when people speak of this church). One person described it being like Noah's ark, 'a place of safety in the midst of storms'. People have the freedom to be themselves as individuals, no matter where they come from or what they believe. There is a recognition of their talents and everyone has the opportunity, and is actively encouraged, to participate and contribute. The fact of pre-existing diversity means there isn't a dominant culture and therefore people are less likely to feel judged or questioned. And there is a strong collective commitment to love as Jesus preached and modelled it. This minority group in a mixed faith area has a real humility alongside confidence in, and boldness to proclaim, the gospel of Jesus Christ.

The call to conversion

I've undergone a process of conversion as I've explored interculturalism. I thought my lifelong exposure to different cultures meant I would find it easy in Leicester to see diversity as a gift and to reflect on the interaction of different cultures. But through my engagement with people like Sunny and churches like All Saints and our IWCs, I've had to face up to the fact I've been in thrall to ethnocentrism and white normativity. It's one thing to say that we are open to other cultures. It's quite another to take up our cross, die to self and be open to receive from God through a person of another culture.

All of this suggests a process of conversion not unlike that recorded in Acts 10 and 11. The story of Peter and Cornelius is well known, but I confess that for many years I read it as an account of the conversion of Cornelius – one of a number of stories recounted in Acts of gentiles becoming followers of Christ. But I was then struck by the fact that the story is recounted twice in great detail – the second time in Acts 11 when Peter describes events to the Council in Jerusalem. Why twice? And why in such detail? It was then that the penny dropped. I realized that the real focus is the conversion of Peter – the disciple who spent so much time with Jesus, who was the first to declare that Jesus was the Messiah (Mark 8.29), who denied Jesus but was then reinstated as one of the foremost disciples (John 21.15 onwards). He had to be converted again to God's purposes for all people: 'I now realise how true it is that God treats everyone the same [..] He accepts people from every nation' (Acts 10.34-35, New International Reader's Version). The story is so significant because it led to a huge shift in the trajectory of the early church, from being a small Jewish sect to becoming a diverse church which within a few decades spread through the Middle East, parts of Europe and Africa.

The point is that Peter was a good Jew, steeped in Jewish traditions, customs, rituals – in short, Jewish culture. And here he is being asked, through a dream, to break certain traditions within his own culture, to overcome his fears and engage with another culture. After his dream Peter went to Cornelius and entered his house, a very public rejection of a part of his culture. Not surprising then, that he was summonsed to give an account of himself to the church leaders in Jerusalem. And while Acts 11 says that his accusers were silenced and then began to praise God, Acts 15 shows that the controversy grew and had to be settled by a meeting of apostles and elders. Peter's conversion was the decisive moment which sparked this process. (The matter was sidelined when the Gentile church grew so large that Jewish heritage followers of Christ were left a tiny minority. Arguably the dispute has never been fully settled, hence the continuing complexity of Jewish–Christian relations). Peter's conversion was the decisive moment which sparked this process.

As mentioned in the Introduction, it took the murder of George Floyd in 2020 and the protests that followed in the USA and around the world, for many church leaders to be 'converted' to the reality of racial injustice in the church and society. For years, one committee after another in the Church of England had written reports on the prejudice faced by many GMH and UKME people. There were calls for action, and a handful of people and churches responded. But overall, the reports fell on deaf ears. However, there are now signs of the first fruits of 'conversion' within the Church of England – a process which is likely to take a long time rather than be a one-off event.

Yet I am also struck that Acts 10 and 11 tell us little of what happened to Cornelius after his conversion. What part did he go on to play in the life of the church? How did he follow Christ as a soldier in the Roman Army? How did he get on with other Christian disciples who were Jewish zealots i.e. revolutionaries? We simply don't know. The focus is on Peter, who at that time was part of the dominant group within the church. Yet history tells us that Peter's conversion was part of the process of the dominant group becoming the marginal group and vice versa. The 'centre' of church activity and theology rapidly shifted from Jerusalem towards Rome and then North Africa.

In a similar way, the centre of today's church has begun shifting from the West towards the Global South. I say 'begun' because even though the church is numerically much stronger in the Global South, the West still has most of the power, largely exercised through finance. While we don't know how this will develop over the coming decades, the vision of intercultural church is one of a multicentred church without dominant and marginal groups. It is a vision of each individual and every cultural group being valued and playing an equal part within their community. And it is a vision of each national church playing an equal part in the global church. It may be naive to think it achievable this side of heaven – history suggests that one hegemony is most likely to be replaced by another – but as we are converted to the other and to God, we can be hopeful that change is possible. For all the mistakes of the past, God is gracious and has not given up on us yet!

Some questions for reflection:

● What have been your experiences of cultural diversity? Have these been positive experiences and/or complex experiences, and why did they feel this way?

● How have you seen others responding to cultural diversity? What has been behind these responses?

● How do you see culture being 'contested' in our society and church?

● Does the example of All Saints Belgrave spark ideas about gifts which can be exchanged?

● What do you think it means to be 'converted' to the gift of the other?

Some suggestions for further reading:

● Anthony Gittens, *Living Mission Interculturally*

● Church Mission Society, Anvil Journal https://churchmissionsociety.org/anvil-journal-theology-and-mission/

● Jon Yates, *Fractured: Why our societies are coming apart and how we put them back together again*

3.   The Gift of the Other

In this chapter, I'll be exploring:

- the variety of gifts that can be given and received;

- seeing ourselves as a gift to others, and the other as a gift to us;

- the history of gift exchange and the dynamic of power involved;

- healthy gift exchange as generous giving, radical receptivity and transformative thanksgiving.

Among the Susu people of West Africa, greeting someone is a form of liturgical dance. One person asks a series of questions which all receive a set response from the other. They then switch places and repeat all the same questions with all the same answers. Only once this ritual is complete can a conversation begin. It goes something like this:

Tana mu xi? (How is the morning?)
Tana yo mu xi. (The morning is fine.)

Tana mu na na? (How are you?)
Tana yo mu na na? (I'm well)

I baba go? (How is your father?)
I na na. (He is well.)

I mama go? (How is your mother?)
I na na. (She is well.)

Denbaya go? (How is your family?)

I na na. (They are well)

Tana mu na na? (How are you?)

Tana yo mu na na? (I'm well.)

It's a little different from the English 'Hello, how are you?' and it often includes physical touch – men will shake hands and then continue to hold hands while the greeting is done (and even beyond that point). This says a lot about different understandings of physical space, contact and time.

When my wife and I moved to Guinea in West Africa and starting living among the Susu people, the greeting ritual was the first thing we had to learn (all of it translated from French, the national language). However, when the greeting is all you know, it can lead to some awkward moments. I remember when I was interrupted in my language learning by a knock at the front door: when I opened the door, I saw a woman with three children – two toddlers either side of her and a small baby strapped to her back in the traditional African way. She greeted me with all the questions and I responded with all the set responses. I then asked her all the questions and she completed the ritual. Having reached the limit of my conversational skills, I did the only thing that I could think of, which was to indicate with my hands that she was welcome to come in and take a seat in our lounge. She did this, a child either side of her, and the baby skilfully manoeuvred from her back onto her lap. Having sat down, she greeted me again and I responded.

We then sat in silence as I wondered what I was supposed to do or say. Should I get her some drinks or food? Had she come seeking help of some kind – in which case, how would she tell me? Should I go and find my language teacher even though he was some distance away?

Sensing my discomfort, she launched once again into the greeting and we danced once more.

Now I was growing really uncomfortable. The silence was deafening. Was I committing some terrible faux pas by not doing or saying something? Would she report this to all the neighbours who would never talk to me again because of my rudeness? I looked at my watch as the silence seemed to go on for eternity.

She smiled at me as she stood up and once again switched the baby onto her back, re-tying the colourful cloth. As she walked to the door, she greeted me one more time. I responded with as much enthusiasm as I could muster, all the while crumbling inside.

As she walked out of the front door, I made a dash for the back door and ran down the lane to find my language teacher. 'What was I supposed to do?' I asked breathlessly, having recounted the event. 'Have I offended her?' I can still remember the smile on his face as he gently reassured me. 'No, no, you are fine,' he said. 'In our culture, it is normal to greet someone new by going to their house, welcoming them and presenting a gift. My guess is that she is too poor to bring a material gift, so she gave you something much more precious. She gave you the gift of her time.'

These words began a journey of exploration for me of what is generally called gift exchange. It had simply never occurred to me that time could be a gift that you offer to someone else. But time is something that we all have, and we can choose how to use it. And for a young mum with three small children, time is a particularly precious gift to lavish on someone else.

The lesson was to come in handy for me, when sometime later I visited a family who had just suffered a bereavement. I discovered that it was normal for the bereaved family to spend around a week at home simply receiving visitors. And what a relief it was to discover that the visitors didn't need to say much, if anything at all. We simply sat with the family in silence. Silence too can be a gift. The theologian Ivan Illich wrote at length about silence, not as the absence of sound, but rather as a form of communication. 'Only the very brave ... dare ... to go back to the helpless silence of being learners and listeners – "the holding of hands of the lovers" – which deep communication may grow. Perhaps it is the one way of being together with others and with the Word in which we have no more foreign accent.'[25]

So, gifts come in all sorts of shapes and sizes. In white, British, middle-class culture, we tend to think of the birthday and Christmas variety, or maybe the flowers and bottle of wine we take when going for dinner at a friend's house. But we also recognize the gift that an artist or musician 'possesses'. We call it a gift because, to some degree or other, we recognize those abilities as coming from a 'higher power'. And so they pass on their gift to us. If you have ever found your soul being stirred by music, or your eyes unable to fully take in the beauty of a piece of art, then you will know this unfathomable gift.

Lewis Hyde's book *The Gift: How the Creative Spirit Transforms the World*[26] is a classic when it comes to exploring the concept of gift. He starts out writing about poetry: 'In sympathy the poet receives (inhales, absorbs) the embodied presences of creation into the self; in pride he [sic] asserts (exhales, emanates) his being out toward others.' And he goes on to explore the complexities of gift-giving touched on here by writer Margaret Atwood in her review of the book: 'Think of "Greeks bearing gifts," a reference to the fatal Trojan horse, and the poisoned apple given to Snow White, not to mention that other apple given to Adam and the wedding gifts that burn Medea's rival to the bone.'[27] This is the double-handedness of gifts.

Hyde's book is still in print forty years after its first publication. However, I would recommend trying to find a first edition – not just because hunting in second hand bookshops is a fun pastime – but because the first edition had a Shaker painting of a basket of apples on the front cover. Hyde explains why:

The Shakers believed that they received their arts as gifts from the spiritual world. Persons who strove to become receptive of songs, dances, paintings, and so forth were said to be 'laboring for a gift,' and the works that they created circulated as gifts within the community. Shaker artists were known as 'instruments'; we know only a few of their names, for in general it was forbidden that they be known to any but the church elders.

However, as Margaret Atwood points out:

This note is followed by a copyright line that, in view of the origins of *Basket of Apples*, reads ironically: '*Basket of Apples* is reprinted through the courtesy of The Shaker Community Inc.' So the community of gift givers has now become incorporated, and its gifts have been transformed to property by the commodity market that now surrounds us on all sides. One of the questions Hyde asks is whether a work of art is changed by the way it is treated – as gift or as commodity for sale. In the case of *Basket of Apples*, I would say not: the word courtesy implies that no money changed hands. But it could have, whereas under the Shaker rules such a thing would have been impossible. Hyde's point is taken.

Hyde explores at length the example of Walt Whitman, one of America's most famous poets. He was described as 'a poet that was selfless without regard for making money and giving his gift to the world and nursing the ill to the point that he would get sick and have headaches.' The final lines of his poem, *Song of the Open Road*, suggest he placed a greater value on friendship or camaraderie than on financial return:

> Camerado, I give you my hand!
>
> I give you my love more precious than money,
>
> I give you myself before preaching or law;
>
> Will you give me yourself? will you come travel with me?
>
> Shall we stick by each other as long as we live?

Such self-giving love is, of course, very Christlike. Yet, as we will explore in the next chapter, it raises questions as to how much we can give out without also taking in. Can we really imitate Christ's *kenosis* (self-giving) or is there a danger of giving so much of ourselves that we end up exhausted and burnt out?

These are just some of the questions raised by gift exchange. The complexities of the topic have long been explored by writers and philosophers (summarized below). It is precisely because of the depth of this exploration that I believe the topic is so relevant to interculturalism. The complexities involve power imbalances – gifts are often given by the weaker party to win favour with the powerful, or they are given by the powerful to ensure the weaker party knows their place. This links to the differentials between cultures mentioned in the last chapter. And gifts have always formed a significant part of colonialism – most colonialists believe they are giving gifts to those they colonize e.g. the gift of civilization or democracy, while those on the receiving end usually have a very different view.

Seeing ourselves and others as a gift

First and foremost, I want to stress that we are a gift – every single one of us. The dignity of our personhood is such that we – as human beings – are a gift. So the newborn baby is a gift, even though they are entirely dependent on others. The older person with dementia is a gift, even though they can't contribute to society in the way they may have done when they were younger. And when I spoke recently to the mother of a non-verbal child who has multiple additional needs and requires 24-hour care, she was at pains to stress to me that she sees her daughter as the most wonderful gift. She was not the daughter that this woman and her husband were expecting when they started on the journey of parenthood, and they had to learn to adjust their expectations. But now, seventeen years on, she was clear that her daughter had transformed her understanding of the nature of love. So, my first question is: can I see myself as a gift? Then I wonder how easy it is to see the other as a gift to me? And then there is the question of the otherness of God who is a gift to us precisely because God is so unlike us.

This recognition of personhood as a gift is important in the field of interculturalism. I am not speaking here of the gifts that people have, but rather the gift that people are. In Genesis 2.18, we hear the first 'not good' of creation (after the list of 'goods' in Chapter 1) – 'It is not good that the man should be alone'. And so God creates a helper (the Hebrew word carries the sense of *ally* or *rescuer*, often used of God). And although the passage goes on to speak of marriage, it is clear from elsewhere in the Bible that family, community and society are also in view. Hence, the African version of Descartes' famous saying, 'I am because we are'. Relationships are key to human flourishing.

There are a whole host of reasons why people may struggle to see themselves as a gift to others. However, it needs to be stated bluntly that colonialism and racism can be primary factors for many. In conversation with a South African school teacher recently, she described just how hard it is to motivate young people 'who have been told all their lives that they are less than human and have nothing to contribute'. This tragically illustrates the way that colonialism is not just about the occupation of other lands but also the pernicious mindset which dehumanizes both colonized and colonizer. There are so many historic examples of explorers referring to the people they encountered as 'savages' – this was the justification for dispossession and slavery – and it continues today in both the blatant racism of some, and the unconscious biases of many. 'We can't be blamed for what our ancestors did!' is the common argument, and there is some truth in this. But when used as an excuse to avoid addressing the legacy of slavery and colonialism, then it is inhumane.

A member of one of our IWCs commented to the researcher from the University of Loughborough that before we could really move forward on interculturalism, we needed to do more to address racism. For people of minoritized cultures to feel safe to share, they need to know that racism is being addressed, not just through formal policies and training, but through all that we do in our churches – discipleship, formation, training, sermons, liturgy, marking Black History Month and so on. Using different channels is important so no one can miss the message.

Another person gave the following feedback:

Before the lockdown, we would have services where we focused on the gospel and people would listen to me, and I would feel empowered and encouraged. But when we went out for lunch or dinner afterwards, people formed cliques/groups and when I tried to join in with white females, they had banter that I didn't really understand, and I told them that I didn't quite understand.

However, they kept talking and there were a lot of inside jokes and I felt excluded. Another example that traumatized me was that once we went out for my birthday, and one of my friends said, 'You should do a birthday speech!' and another person said, 'No, she's going to blush.' Then another church leader said, 'Even if she blushes, we won't be able to see it anyway because she's so dark.' Everyone laughed and I laughed too because I didn't want to cause a commotion, but I have experienced things in social settings where I felt like the focus of mockery […] I was working with lovely people, but people would come up to me and said that I spoke really good English. I asked, 'What would you expect me to speak?' and they would say, 'No I'm just surprised you speak such good English.' I kept hearing comments like that, and I've been hearing comments like that throughout my journey, which makes me uncomfortable.

Another person said that being put 'in a box' was disabling. There is a tension to be navigated between acknowledging and giving space to cultural difference without labelling or making assumptions: 'People wanted to emphasize my otherness as a way of reminding me that I did not belong to their story'; 'In the past I tried to fit in and now I don't want to fit in, I just want to be myself.' The emotional labour is often put on the shoulders of minoritized people – the sense that 'you need to demonstrate why we should let you join us'. Another individual in the focus group commented, 'There is a culture of gatekeeping rather than gate-opening … If you are not invited to house groups, you are excluded. Ladies' walking group, for example. I have never been invited. And I know in the English culture, you go when you are invited.'

From the moment they arrive in this country, asylum seekers and refugees are often given the message (spoken or unspoken) that they are a nuisance, a drain on our scarce resources and unwanted – everything, in fact, which is the opposite of a gift. Many describe how they feel themselves stripped of their dignity and infantilized. 'All we want to do is contribute,' said one asylum seeker to me when I visited the hotel where he and his family were being housed, 'but people think we have nothing to contribute. We are not even seen as human.'

So how does the church, the 'new society' created by God, show that every person is a gift? I believe the focal point is the Eucharist. At its simplest, the liturgy reminds us of all that God has done for us (collectively and individually), carefully holding together our sinfulness and unworthiness, and God's grace and mercy. Yet on a much deeper level, as expressed by former Archbishop of Canterbury, Rowan Williams: 'the essence of the church is communion in and with the triune being of God through participating in the relation of the Son and the Father through the Eucharist.'[28] So in baptism and Holy Communion, our human dignity is affirmed as we are drawn into the life of the Trinity. And as we are then commissioned as disciples of Christ, there are a thousand possibilities for how we (the church) can show by our actions that we value people for who they are – from practical help with basic necessities, food and furniture, through to English language classes and places for people to express their own culture (whether in food, music, dance or hospitality). Of course, we will want to value their skills and talents also (more about that in a moment) but the key message is 'we value you as a person'.

We are all 'gifted'

In addition to the gift of ourselves, all of us also have particular gifts, abilities and talents. Some we are born with, some are related to our personality, our experiences, our upbringing and our training, and some are described in the Bible as 'gifts of the Spirit' or 'spiritual gifts', related to building up the Body of Christ.

Again, it is not straightforward to identify these gifts in ourselves or others. So much will depend on early life experiences – have we been told that we are 'gifted' and given lots of opportunities to develop these gifts? Or have we been told that we will never amount to anything, with our abilities ridiculed? Many who come to the UK from other countries find it hard to share their gifts. They may not be recognized, for example academic qualifications from a foreign university which are perceived as not carrying the same weight as those from a UK university, or long years spent working in a particular job that now count for nothing as retraining is required to be able to do the same job in the UK. Some may find it hard to know how to share their gifts because of the different culture e.g. a style of music which may be regarded as a novelty in the West and is not really taken seriously.

Confidence can also be a real issue. One leader in an IWC commented to the Loughborough University researcher: 'We have BAME people involved in our services but they seem to require a bit more encouragement to step up, lead prayers, and they seem to be lacking in confidence. They find it harder to respond to leading up-front services... the Nigerian lady on the PCC took a long time to speak in meetings. It's a learning curve. She was actually quite reluctant to come on, I pushed her to.'

Then there are the practicalities of life – whether to do with immigration status, which can have a profound effect on confidence – or those factors which can apply to people of any background: working long hours, zero hour contracts which mean there is always a pressure to be working to be earn enough money, doing shift work (and therefore not being available at the same time every week), juggling childcare and other family responsibilities. There can be so many practical obstacles to people sharing their gifts.

I'm often struck that the Church of England puts huge resources into helping people discern whether they are being called to ordination in God's church.[29] In part, this is about discerning their gifts through their own self-reflection, through references from those they have worked with, and those who know them well, as well as observations of their contributions as volunteers in church. In recent years, we have started to broaden this process to include wider discernment about someone's calling or vocation – whether to lay ministry in the church, or to some role in the community or wider society. We have also begun to wake up to the fact that people from different cultures face additional challenges in discerning their vocation within a second culture. Too often in the past we have expected people to fit white British norms as they go through the process.

As just one example (admittedly from another continent), this quote from an Asian American gives a sense of what's involved for people of different cultures (remembering that within most Asian cultures, honouring parents and elders is one of the highest values).

As a college student at a Christian conference, I picked up a new book called *Following Jesus Without Dishonouring Your Parents*. In baggy jean shorts and an oversized T-shirt, I read a few chapters while sitting on the floor next to the book table, not yet wanting to commit my few dollars to the purchase. But reading it, I felt seen; I didn't connect with everything, but I connected with many things. So I bought the book and referred to it often as I finished college and started an engineering job – navigating career, calling, and my relationship with my parents. Reading the book helped me name and process my experiences around identity.[30]

The church urgently needs many more resources like this, ideally written specifically for the UK context and the variety of cultures present here. We need much greater diversity in our leadership so that everyone can dare to believe 'this could be my calling too'. So, for church leaders, this means dedicating time to pray with, and talk to people about their gifting and vocation.[31] It means finding out about their hopes, dreams and what may be holding them back from exploring these. There is no substitute for spending time with people in this way although it must be acknowledged that people will not always want to talk about painful experiences of racism and prejudice – and should not be forced to recount and relive these experiences. Similarly, church leaders may need to act as a 'lightning rod' when there is backlash or resistance to embracing different cultures. We need to be prepared to stand firmly behind those of minoritized backgrounds and stay committed to the journey. Finally, there is also a need to plan the 'stepping stones' which will enable someone to explore their gifts and build their confidence, particularly if they are working in a second culture. Giving people opportunities for ministry (related to their gifting, and not just as tokenism) is all-important. And a mentor can be really helpful in this process,[32] ideally someone from a similar cultural background who can act as a guide and interpreter (in the broadest sense).

Learning from the history of gift exchange

As far as we are aware, most ancient societies were built on some form of gift exchange. However, what constitutes a gift, how it is passed on, and what is offered in return, has changed greatly through history and still varies between different cultures. Greek warriors expected their superiors to give them an equitable share of the plunder they helped to win – military service should be rewarded with honourable gifts. In return, Greek leaders expected loyalty and continuing military service as a grateful response to the gifts received. The same was true in Rome, where patrons expected their clients to return faithful service and to express public, exuberant gratitude, thus enhancing the status of the patron.

By contrast, in contemporary England, gifts generally operate in the sphere of our private lives – everything else is governed by the state or the market – so gratitude is more typically understood as a sentiment expressed verbally. Although there is still some sense of an expectation of a return (if I invite you to dinner, I might hope that you will return the invitation at some point), we are a very long way from a society governed and structured on formal gifts. So why the dramatic difference? How did we arrive at this very divergent understanding of gift exchange?

In his book *Gratitude: An Intellectual History*,[33] Peter Leithart chronicles the history of gratitude (the way we respond to a gift) in great detail, including the role of Christianity in the changes over time. His argument is that there have been two basic forms of gift exchange – one which can be pictured as a circle and one which can be pictured as a straight line. In circular terms, a donor gives a gift or does a favour for a beneficiary, and the beneficiary is expected to return a gift or favour at some future time to the donor. As he explains:

To put it 'algebraically', A gives B to C, and A expects C to give D back. The second clause of the sentence summarises what is meant by 'gratitude' in ancient societies … Circles of gift and gratitude bound together the aristocracy of Republican Rome, and in Imperial Rome, circles of gift, and response bound officials and the Roman people to the generous emperor, cities to their provincial governors, provinces to the capital.

However, these bonds of obligation could be suffocating and inevitably created cliques of those bound together by particular obligations. The expectations were so high that to break them a person risked being ostracized from society – or even being punished as a criminal. One's status, health, wealth and reputation depended on fulfilling the obligations. For a brief period, Athens experimented with a political system that detached the cycles of giving and receiving from institutions of power. Between 462 and 322 BC, Athens put in place a system whereby those in authority were expected to use their power for the common good of the city, rather than for the particular good of their circle of friends. Gratitude took the form of civic patriotism, rather than loyalty to kin, clan or clique. Even though the experiment didn't last long, it did open the door for some creative thinking. Aristotle imagined the 'magnanimous man' who, although he would repay the gift, would do so as quickly as possible so as to remain free of dependency and obligations. Seneca, in his work *De beneficiis (On benefits)* also imagined a more linear approach to gifts by encouraging good men to give like gods, even to the ungrateful, in the hope that gifts will induce the ungrateful to turn grateful.

Yet Jesus introduced something even more radical. Jesus tells his disciples to give without thinking of a return, and to imitate their Heavenly Father in giving to the ungrateful and even to enemies (e.g. Luke 6.35). Indeed, Jesus gave priority to those who could not repay – the poorest in society – and he encouraged his followers to give without anxiety about depleting their resources because of their heavenly Father's infinite resources. In addition, Jesus taught that we should give in secret because we are not seeking the praise or obligations of humans but we are confident that God, who sees what we do in secret, will reward us (Matthew 6.4). It is easy for modern ears to miss the radical nature of this teaching in its context.

For Paul, the proper reception of gifts includes the giving of thanks to God and the right use of the gift. As Leithart puts it:

> Giving appears to be a linear, selfless, sacrifice, and gratitude does not come back to the giver, but branches out as the gift disseminates forever. Romans naturally regarded early Christians as antisocial ingrates. Christians broke the circle, and began to unravel the fabric of Roman society and politics ... Christianity freed people from onerous personal bonds by defining gratitude as *right use* of the gift, rather than gratitude as *return* ... Gifts flow on and on, but the generous, cheerful giver can hope for a return [because] the line of the unrequited gift, and the branching line of grateful dissemination, is circumscribed by a circle of infinite diameter. The circle is infinite because God is the source of *every* gift ... also because the promised return does not necessarily happen in time; it may be required at the final judgement.

This helps to explain some of the subtleties of Paul's teaching about generosity and gratitude in the New Testament. Arguably, the collecting of gifts from one congregation to pass them on to another, was for him second in priority only to sharing the gospel of Jesus Christ (remembering that gifts include the sending of people and encouragement as well as financial support). And as John Barclay argues in *Paul and the Gift*,[34] since the Greek word *charis* can be translated either as 'gift' or 'grace', there is a direct link between Paul's emphasis on the grace of God and his teaching about gift-giving. Indeed, Barclay's work is extremely helpful in unpacking what Paul might have meant by the term 'gift' (in his own historical and sociological context) and contrasting this with the popular understanding of grace today.

Leithart claims that the medieval world which took shape in the ruins of the Roman Empire, although still governed by the narrow circle of gift and return moving between 'lords' and 'vassals', was also marked by the Christian linear gift exchange and the 'infinite circle' which includes God. New institutions such as hospitals sprang up, modelling the linearity of Christian giving. There was also a twist on this theme as monks became known as 'God's poor': donations to monasteries were regarded as 'alms', so donors viewed their giving as storing up riches in heaven. This was eventually taken to such excess, with the 'donation' seen as guaranteeing heavenly reward, that it became a trigger for the Protestant Reformation. Indulgences had become a form of commerce, and the mass had become a work which 'won' favour with God rather than being viewed as thanksgiving for a gift already received. The reformers therefore paved the way for the modern era's linear and altruistic view of gifts.

It was not long after this that money replaced gifts as the bond of service in Europe. Kings began to pay soldiers rather than using retainers to whom they were personally tied with bonds of gift and gratitude. This led to something of a political crisis, with many wondering what could hold society together if not gifts and gratitude. Shakespeare expressed the anxieties of the time in tragedies of ingratitude like *King Lear* and *Coriolanus*.

Eventually this new political vision was clearly articulated by John Locke. As Leithart explains:

From Locke on, liberal political theory is founded on the deliberate uncoupling of relationships of benefit and gratitude from the laws, procedures, and practices of politics. Civil order was founded on consent, and had to run according to regular rules and processes, free from the disruption of gifts. Locke's theory did not 'privatise' gratitude, which would imply that there was a pre-existing private space into which gratitude was confined. Rather, Locke's theory constituted the private sphere as a 'space' where circles of favour, thanks, and return favours operated as they did before, but without touching public order.

And what Locke did for political theory, Adam Smith did for economic theory. There is no mention of gratitude in *Wealth of Nations*. Yet in his book *Theory of Moral Sentiments*, many pages are devoted to considering gratitude in the social, domestic or private life. This is the first description of gratitude as a moral sentiment. As Leithart says, 'it moves from the realm of ethics to the realm of etiquette'. And with other Enlightenment writers such as Kant, we get the first glimpse of altruistic gifts or what has sometimes been called 'pure gift' i.e. giving simply for the good of the other. Since that time, the argument has raged – is there really such a thing as a 'pure gift'? Or do we always expect some return, even if it is simply the warm glow inside from feeling that we have done good?

It was in this context that Marcel Mauss, in 1925, published his now famous book *The Gift*.[35] Mauss was a French sociologist and anthropologist, who drew on the research of other anthropologists in places such as the Pacific Islands. Mauss was the first to see that in these societies, as in many ancient societies, gift-giving and gift-receiving was a 'total social fact' – an institution, practice and ritual that embodied the entirety of a culture. The practice contained religious, juridical, economic and moral elements, as well as being related to politics and family life. It 'impregnated' the whole of society. However, he was also very clear that giving was competitive – people would try to outdo each other in the largesse of their gift, thus proving their status and power – and it was done in expectation of a return gift.

Mauss' work has spawned a whole body of other literature. As an example, Jacques Derrida directly engages with Mauss in his own philosophical exploration of gift.[36] He believes that in focusing on gift *exchange*, Mauss directly contradicts the reality of gift which, in order to be true gift (or pure gift), cannot have any expectation of a return. The moment a gift is acknowledged as such, it loses the character of gift and becomes commerce. Such deconstruction doesn't however take us very far. John Milbank[37] rejects Derrida's analysis and focuses instead on the relationship between giver and receiver. He uses the example of lovers who delight to give each other gifts – in such a relationship, the exchange of gifts does not corrupt the gift. So too in wider society, gifts must be purged of the competitive and honour-driven features that characterized gifts in ancient societies. Milbank sees this happening in the church:

> The exchange of gifts is what constitutes the church as a body made up of Jews and Gentiles: the Romans are exhorted to acknowledge the gift of the announcement of God which they owe to the Jews and their law, not only by words but also by material almsgiving to the poor in Jerusalem. The gospel, as it shapes the church, announces the possibility of purified gift exchange … in 'perpetual Eucharist' – that is, a community living through the offering of the gift given to us of God himself in the flesh.

I hope that this lightning-fast tour of the history of gift exchange will at least have given a glimpse of the richness of this theme for our exploration of interculturalism (among other things). There are many possible implications, but I offer a few in the hope that this can begin a wider conversation.

(1)   Generous giving

In Western society, gift exchange has been very much relegated to the private sphere (indeed we have laws to keep it out of politics – though the effectiveness of these laws is open to debate!) However, despite the effects of globalization, there are many societies around the world that still have a broader understanding of gift exchange. So, while our historical survey has highlighted many of the pitfalls, it is noteworthy that Jesus didn't dismiss the gift exchange which operated in his society. Rather, he extended it in a radically new way – give to those who can't repay you, he teaches, because your heavenly Father, who has infinite resources, will repay you. And in case this sounds a little like 'prosperity gospel' teaching, it is worth pointing out that this passage in Matthew's Gospel includes Jesus' teaching on prayer: 'Give us this day our daily bread.' For a very interesting take on what this means in a world of such inequality see Musa Dube's article *Praying the Lord's Prayer in a Global Economic Era*.[38]

Relegating gift exchange to the private sphere means that we have, to some degree at least, lost a sense of the way in which the circulation of gifts creates community. If we can take the onerous obligations out of the system, there is still a sense in which gift giving creates a 'feeling bond' (Lewis Hyde) between giver and receiver. These connections, both bonding (people like us) and bridging (people unlike us), deepen community. Furthermore, when done in a healthy way, the circulation of gifts grows communication and trust, further vital elements of social capital (the term used by sociologists to gauge the strength of relationships within society).

To go back to my opening story, among the Susu people (and elsewhere in Africa) it is normal to welcome someone new with a gift – whether the gift of time or the gift which a number of our other neighbours brought, a live chicken! This immediately made us feel welcome while also creating a 'feeling bond' with people whose culture was very different to our own. Of course, it was complicated, because it immediately raised the question of what we were going to give, or do, in return (the short-term answer was to cook the chickens so we could have a shared meal after church on Sunday!) But if we are overwhelmed by the complications such that we stop giving, then both we and the community as a whole are diminished. We will return to this idea of 'healthy' giving in a moment, but for now I note that if we want to develop intercultural communities then generosity and gift giving are essential. This is undoubtedly an area where those of us from Western cultures can learn from our brothers and sisters from other cultures for whom this is much more part of their normal practice.

(2)   Radical receptivity

This leads to a second point, which concerns our willingness to receive from others, and how this is done in a 'healthy' way. I remember hearing an African bishop comment some years ago that 'the problem with the West is that you haven't learnt to receive'. It is, I think, a fair comment. Our models of mission generally focus on giving – whether we give the gospel of Jesus Christ, practical aid or advocacy. This is important, as I've just said, but the reality is that among the hundreds of books written on mission which assume the model of giving, there are very few which work with a model of receiving.

Al Barrett's recent books are an exception – his PhD thesis was published as *Interrupting the Church's Flow: A radically receptive political theology in the urban margins*,[39] and he then went on to write a shorter, more accessible version (with Ruth Harley), *Being Interrupted: Reimagining the Church's Mission from the Outside, In*.[40] His central argument in both of these is the need for 'radical receptivity' which he describes as 'opening ourselves intentionally to receive and be changed by the gifts and challenges of our "others"'. He goes on to explain,

---

I am not proposing radical receptivity as a universal prescription … Radical receptivity is not for everybody, for every situation. It is dependent on context, and on a careful analysis and negotiation of the complex power differentials within our relationships. For a white, middle-class, able-bodied, heterosexual, male Anglican priest like me, it's pretty clear that I'm a beneficiary from structural privilege in multiple aspects of my identity, and so my advocacy of radical receptivity is addressed most strongly to myself – and to multiply-privileged people like me. But what Anthony Reddie calls 'complex subjectivity' reminds us that it is possibly to be privileged in some aspects of our identity (and in our particular position in a particular situation), and disadvantaged in others …

Radical receptivity demands, then, an ongoing alertness to the power dynamics of the situations and interactions in which we find ourselves. Such an alertness takes effort – always, I reckon. For friends and neighbours whose bodies or backgrounds are often rendered 'other', years spent with this alertness to power being an unavoidable aspect of life may well have already proved thoroughly draining. But for those of us who have benefited from structural privilege (whose 'whiteness', for example, has been rendered largely invisible in most of our social contexts), this alertness may well feel, to begin with at least, like a very under-used muscle that is suddenly being asked to work.

Barrett outlines a number of other reasons why many of us may find this radical receptivity difficult. Among them is the fact that those of us who are privileged often find it easier to identify with Jesus in the gospel stories, rather than with the recipients of Jesus' healing and help. In effect, we put ourselves in the positions of saviour, rescuer and provider, rather than those in need of help. Change, he suggests, will come from the edges, from those who know they are in need of healing.

This is a helpful contribution to current thinking about mission, and builds on the work of those, such as Sam Wells,[41] who have written on mission as 'being with'. Personally, I think that gift exchange offers a more mutual approach, one which retains a focus on sharing the good news of Jesus Christ whatever our status and culture, while also accepting that it is undoubtedly the case that many of us in the West need to learn how to receive as well as give.

As an example, (which will sound trivial but in reality asks profound questions as to how the church is governed) in his book *Is God Colour-Blind? Insights from Black Theology for Christian Ministry*, Anthony Reddie recalls being overwhelmed by stacks of paperwork at the annual Methodist Conference. It led him to reflect on the very different cultural approaches to organizing and discerning consensus within large groups of people: 'This method of producing a "collective mind on governance", however, elevates one way of knowing and disregards other methods of knowing, namely the proverbial wisdom of African-Caribbean folk [and many other cultures], perhaps closer in kind to how Jesus shared his knowledge – through parables and stories.'[42]

I confess to having a lot of sympathy with Reddie – the Church of England loves to write reports! But this is a serious point about our ways of working. We talk a lot about discernment and wise decision-making – but why do we think that report writing is the best way to do this? Is it because we default to a particular cultural model – the way we've been trained? Is it because it can feel very risky to 'let go' of what is familiar and give control to someone else who operates in a different cultural form? 'Radical receptivity' is about daring to open ourselves to very different ways of doing things.

Having said this, I also repeat what I wrote earlier – this is not to suggest that we descend into complete relativism, accepting everything other cultures have to offer. There are some 'universal' values (just as we have universal human rights), and there are some things which are core to the identity of the Church of England, but there are many others which are culturally conditioned and need to be critically assessed to see if other ways might be more befitting Christian mission in Britain in the twenty-first century.

(3) Transformative thanksgiving

Milbank is right to say that gifts 'must be purged of competitive, agonistic and honour-driven features that characterized gifts in ancient and tribal societies'. His focus on relationship is important as we consider how this is done. It's not that our motives for giving or receiving have to be pure (can they ever be?), but if we really want the best for someone and if we really delight in the gift, then this will go a long way in overcoming the pitfalls of gift exchange.

This emphasis on relationship is vitally important, and it includes our relationship with the source of all good gifts – God. Leithart's argument about the 'infinite circle' which also includes God, suggests that, whatever our motives, and however strong our relationships, it is the inclusion of God which truly sanctifies the exchange. Surely this is why the Bible is so full of exhortations to give thanks to God – from numerous Old Testament laws, including those concerning the thanksgiving offering and tithe, to countless Psalms; from Jesus' assumption that his followers would be regularly offering gifts at the altar (Matthew 5.23), to the New Testament writers' repeated encouragement to give thanks to God (arguably aimed at gentile believers who would not have been familiar with the centrality of thanksgiving within Judaism). 2 Corinthians 9.11 speaks of this larger circle – God as the origin of all gifts, and these gifts then being disseminated, resulting in thanksgiving to God: 'You will be enriched in every way so that you can be generous on every occasion, and through us your generosity will result in thanksgiving to God'.

The climax of teaching on thanksgiving is surely the Eucharist, the central act of Christian worship. 'Transformation' can be understood in various ways in this context (in what sense do the bread and wine 'become' the body and blood of Jesus?), yet the whole liturgy, from opening acclamation to post-communion prayer, benediction and dismissal can be seen as transformative for the church. This is usually viewed in terms of unity – the great thanksgiving prayer (*sursum corda*, 'lift up your hearts') is an offering of ourselves to God in remembrance (*anamnesis*) of all that God has done for us; the invocation (*epiclesis*) is a prayer for the sanctification of both the bread and wine and the people: 'Send the Holy Spirit on your people and gather into one in your kingdom all who share this one bread and one cup,' (Eucharistic Prayer B). And it is this action of the Holy Spirit which unites us with God and one another. In *The Go-Between God* (recently reprinted), John V. Taylor speaks of the Holy Spirit as the one who works in the spaces between us, generating communion, and enabling the giving and receiving of gifts in a manner that replicates (in a limited way) the giving and receiving within the trinity and within the Eucharist. Furthermore, Henri Nouwen, in a moving set of reflections on the Eucharist, speaks of the transformation of our resentments into gratitude:

The word 'Eucharist' means literally 'act of thanksgiving'. To celebrate the Eucharist and to live a Eucharistic life has everything to do with gratitude. Living Eucharistically is living life as a gift, a gift for which one is grateful. But gratitude is not the most obvious response to life, certainly not when we experience life as a series of losses! Still, the great mystery we celebrate in the Eucharist and live in a Eucharistic life is precisely that through mourning our losses we come to know life as a gift.[43]

So, as well as generous giving and radical receptivity, it is my belief that transformative thanksgiving is essential if we are to have an approach to intercultural gift exchange which honours God and respects our cultural identities. The Eucharist is the central act of Christian worship because in it we receive (radically) the grace and gift of God, and are sent out to give (generously) to the world. Thus, in the regular celebration of Holy Communion, we are presented again and again with a model of healthy gift exchange.

In the next two chapters we will consider what this looks like in terms of practice, firstly in the area of hospitality and the questions of who is host, who is guest and what is being exchanged, and then in terms of intercultural theology where I focus in particular on liturgy (since the Anglican church has always believed that we express our theology in liturgy).

Some questions for reflection:

- A mapping exercise: on a large piece of paper draw the network of your family, friends, work colleagues and other networks. Once you have drawn these, reflect on the different gifts that you exchange with each person/group? Think about the wide variety of different types of gift. How are these exchanged? How are they acknowledged/reciprocated?

- Have you experienced the negative side of gift exchange? What reflections do you have on power dynamics within such exchanges?

- How do you and your church seek to practice generous giving and radical receptivity?

- How have you experienced thanksgiving as being transformative?

Some suggestions for further reading:

- Lewis Hyde, *The Gift: How the Creative Spirit Transforms the World*

- Peter Leithart, *Gratitude: An Intellectual History*

- Nick Spencer, 'Human as Gift' *https://comment.org/human-as-gift/*

'Half-time talk' —
The Gift of Hospitality

By Bishop Saju Muthalaly

Hospitality has a unique place, I believe, in intercultural gift exchange. On one hand, the practice of hospitality is something we in Britain can receive as a gift from other cultures where it is more deeply embedded, like my own country of origin, India. But hospitality is also a channel through which all other gifts, including the gift of ourselves, can be given and received. And, through practising hospitality – welcoming the stranger – we can be led deeper into the heart of a God who is both guest and host.

There is an ancient Sanskrit saying in India, 'Atithi Devo Bhava', which encapsulates the essence of Indian hospitality. It means 'a guest is God's own reflection'; literally *Atithi* means someone without a calendar, which is to say that the stranger arrives at your door at any time. This saying reflects the belief commonly held in India, and other parts of the world too, that guests are a blessing and to be treated with the utmost respect and care. Looking after guests is akin to serving the divine.

This, of course, is a deeply biblical idea. In Genesis 18 and 19, both Abraham and Lot are tested to see whether they will show hospitality to strangers, who are in fact God's messengers. Abraham is sitting by the great trees of Mamre in the heat of the day when he notices three strangers approaching. He immediately runs out to meet them, bows before them and asks if he may have the honour of serving them referring to them as 'my lord' and himself as their 'servant'. He and Sarah prepare them a meal and it is then that the elderly couple receive the news that within a year, they shall have a son. Reflecting on this story, the writer of Hebrews reminds the early Christians: 'Do not neglect to show hospitality to strangers, for by doing that some have entertained angels without knowing it.' (Hebrews 13.2)

Abraham himself receives hospitality from Melchizedek who brings bread and wine (a precursor of the Eucharist) to Abraham after he defeats the coalition of kings under Chedorlaomer. Melchizedek blesses Abraham in the name of 'God Most High'. Here we have Abraham, the patriarch of God's people, the man through whom all nations will be blessed, himself receiving a blessing from a priest and king shrouded in mystery. This incident is a reminder that God is not only at work in and through Abraham, but in all peoples and at all times. It is this which makes intercultural gift exchange so important in seeking to know and love God more.

Like Abraham, Christ both receives and gives hospitality. Jesus' ministry is bookended, in the Gospel of John, by roles of both guest (the Wedding at Cana) and host (at the Last Supper). Throughout Jesus' ministry, he and his disciples depended on the hospitality of strangers, and much of the scandal which dogged them stemmed from whose hospitality Jesus accepted. By eating with 'sinners and tax collectors', he appeared to identify with them, while the Pharisees were fastidious about maintaining the boundaries between difference. Jesus' disciples were also commanded to give hospitality e.g. by feeding the 5,000 as recorded in Matthew 14.13-21, Mark 6.31-44, Luke 9.12-17 and John 6.1-14. They were also commanded to receive it:

As you go, proclaim the good news, 'The kingdom of heaven has come near.' Cure the sick, raise the dead, cleanse the lepers, cast out demons. You received without payment; give without payment. Take no gold, or silver, or copper in your belts, no bag for your journey, or two tunics, or sandals, or a staff; for labourers deserve their food. Whatever town or village you enter, find out who in it is worthy, and stay there until you leave. (Matthew 10.7-11)

This passage, like the story of Lydia's conversion in Acts, suggests that offering hospitality is a proper response to receiving the gift of the gospel: 'A certain woman named Lydia, a worshipper of God, was listening to us; she was from the city of Thyatira and a dealer in purple cloth. The Lord opened her heart to listen eagerly to what was said by Paul. When she and her household were baptized, she urged us, saying, "If you have judged me to be faithful to the Lord, come and stay at my home."' (Acts 16.14-15)

But it is not just how we receive hospitality, but how and to whom we show it which can serve as a mirror, reflecting back to us the depth and nature of our faith. In the parable of the sheep and the goats (Matthew 25.31-46), Jesus describes hospitality as what sets apart one from the other. The goats are punished because Christ, as manifest in 'the least of these', 'was hungry and you gave me no food, I was thirsty and you gave me nothing to drink, I was a stranger and you did not welcome me, naked and you did not give me clothing, sick and in prison and you did not visit me.' In showing hospitality we are expressing our faith in two truths. First, that nothing can remove or reduce the image of God in a person – no wrongdoing, no creed, no controversies. Whatever they have done and whoever they are, they have inviolable dignity and worth. And second, the generosity of God, from which we have received everything we have.

Hospitality as core to Christian discipleship is a profound theme which runs throughout Indian Christian theology – and I hope it is a gift which the Church of England will receive.

Hospitality in Indian and British culture

When I think of Indian hospitality, the first thing that comes to mind is the greeting 'Namaste', which is often translated as 'I bow to you' or 'the divine in me bows to the divine in you' – hence why it is said with a slight bow with hands joined together. It essentially says to the stranger or guest, 'I see you with respect and reverence', and when the guest says it back, they are also communicating their gratitude and showing honour to the host. So there is a humility and a recognition of equality and inherent dignity in this everyday greeting.

Of course, food is a central part of Indian hospitality. I can still find excellent examples of that in the Hindu and Sikh temples in Leicester, our 'Golden Mile', or Indian festivals. For instance, most Sikh gurdwaras offer 'langar', a community kitchen which serves meals to all free of charge, regardless of religion, caste, gender, economic status or ethnicity.

I also think of the way Christianity is said to have first reached India, through St Thomas, because of the hospitality which had been shown to Cochin Jews. The Cochin Jews settled in the area of India where I was born, Kerala, perhaps following the destruction of the first temple in the Siege of Jerusalem in 587 BC. The Cochin Jews were blessed with recognition and rights by the rulers of India – they were granted permission 'as long as the world, sun and moon endure' to live freely, build synagogues and own property 'without conditions attached'.[44] It is believed that St Thomas arrived in India in the first century, looking for the Jewish community which already existed there, to share with them the gospel. The Nasrani Christians, or St Thomas Christians, in Kerala trace their origins to those among the Cochin Jews who received his message.

I learned true hospitality from my mother. My mother was a nurse in a leprosy hospital two kilometres from Bangalore railway station. She would regularly, at great sacrifice to herself, host relatives and often strangers as well, who were looking for a better life in that city. Now my parents live on the southwest coast of India, with very faithful Hindu people as neighbours. Every day, the mother or the son from next door will check in on my parents to see if they are okay. Sometimes my mother gives them peppers, nutmeg or mangoes if they're in season. But, while there is an element of exchange going on, it isn't expected. It is more the case that an honourable person in Indian culture would naturally seek the wellbeing of their elderly neighbours.

This is quite different to the way hospitality is understood and practised in British culture. Here, hospitality often means serving a meal, holding a party or having someone to stay the night. And it is often a transactional or contractual exchange: the act of hospitality is a sign of friendship and trust already built, or there is an expectation that the invitation will be returned. The transaction is even clearer in the 'hospitality industry', where meals, drinks and accommodation are exchanged for money and divorced from any sense of relationship.

Coming to Britain can be quite a shock to people who have grown up in cultures where hospitality is widely practiced. The feeling of being invisible or unwanted can create a barrier to hearing the Christian message – if people experience hostility from the culture it has shaped, then they may understandably question who the God revealed in Christ is to them.

When such sacred gifts have been commercialized, I believe it is the task of discipleship to recover and redeem them. When I was vicar of St Mark's, Gillingham, there was one year when I put aside vision statements and mission strategies and focused on building relationships. 'This year,' I said, 'the only thing we have to do is feed 5,000 people as a church. But don't just invite your best friend or your family member; invite somebody else who you normally would not spend time with for a meal.' It was challenging and beautiful and all part of what Christine Pohl calls 'recovering hospitality as a Christian tradition'.[45] After all, it was Christ who first commanded:

When you give a luncheon or a dinner, do not invite your friends or your brothers or your relatives or rich neighbours, in case they may invite you in return, and you would be repaid. But when you give a banquet, invite the poor, the crippled, the lame, and the blind. And you will be blessed, because they cannot repay you, for you will be repaid at the resurrection of the righteous. (Luke 14.12-14)

Responding to God's hospitality

Why does Jesus say that? What's so wrong about being invited back for another dinner party? The answer, I think, is because we are called to pass on the gift which we have received from God; we are not the instigator of the act of hospitality, and so we are not looking for it to be 'balanced out'.

Throughout the Bible, hospitality is an act of grace: an invitation into the privileges of community for those who would otherwise not have the right to it. Outsiders are treated as insiders. God tells the ancient Israelites: 'When an alien resides with you in your land, you shall not oppress the alien. The alien who resides with you shall be to you as the citizen among you; you shall love the alien as yourself, for you were aliens in the land of Egypt' (Leviticus 19.33-34). Because the Israelites received unearned blessings from God – notably in the form of rescue out of Egypt – those blessings are to be shared freely.

Receiving salvation through God, in the sense of rescue or healing, is a common theme across the Hebrew and Christian Bible. Rahab, for instance, is brought into the Israelite family and saved from the destruction which befalls Jericho in return for hiding the Israelite spies and refusing to surrender them to the king (Joshua 2). In 2 Kings 4, a miraculous chain of events is set into motion by the hospitality of the Shunammite woman. It starts by her regularly offering meals to Elisha. Then she suggests to her husband: 'Let us make a small roof chamber with walls, and put there for him a bed, a table, a chair, and a lamp, so that he can stay there whenever he comes to us.' Having often accepted the Shunammite woman's hospitality, Elisha asks his servant what he can offer in return. As the couple are old and without child, Elisha declares that by that time next year, they will have a son. Elisha goes on to bring that son back from the dead and help the family escape a seven-year famine.

In the New Testament, we see Jesus inviting himself to the house of Zacchaeus, the tax-collector, and while the crowds grumble 'He has gone to be the guest of one who is a sinner', the honour which Jesus shows to Zacchaeus inspires a full repentance. Zacchaeus immediately gives half of his possessions to the poor and promises to pay back anyone he has cheated four times the amount. 'Jesus said to him, "Today salvation has come to this house, because he too is a son of Abraham. For the Son of Man came to seek out and to save the lost."' (Luke 19.9-10) If salvation is about being brought into God's family as much as it is about being forgiven our sin, then we should not be surprised to see this made manifest in acts of hospitality.

For we who are Christians, hospitality is an image of our salvation in another sense also — because we are redeemed by being in Christ. God takes into himself those who do not deserve the privileges of sonship and blesses us as though we did. Having been given 'every spiritual blessing' in Christ (Ephesians 1.3), how could we withhold anything from our sister or brother? Showing hospitality is, therefore, an expression of what Martyn calls transformative thanksgiving – we give from a profound sense of what we have already received.

If we want to become more like Christ, we cannot help but become more hospitable, because hospitality is rooted into the very essence of God. The Trinity itself is a community of perfect love. Each of the members pour their complete self into the other, and each is completely open to the other. God's acts of creation and then incarnation are outworkings of that desire to share God's self, even when we humans make for bad house-guests and neighbours. Even when it means entering into the depths of our hell to redeem us. So learning from other cultures in which hospitality plays a more central role than in Britain is not a matter of cultural relativism or appropriation – it is a way by which we can recover a form of worship which God has always called on us to offer.

Hospitality as the medium for gift exchange

Hospitality in the sense of shared meals and physical acts of welcome are often an expression of intercultural gift exchange. One of our pioneering IWCs here in Leicester puts on two or three cultural celebration events a year, to reflect and honour the different origins of their members. Together they have celebrated Nowruz (Persian New Year) and hosted Kurdish and Romanian celebrations. These events give members from that particular culture an opportunity to introduce their fellow worshippers to the stories, traditions, food and music from their country of origin. In other words, they are offering, as gifts to the rest of the gathering, parts of a culture which they dearly cherish. In receiving and respecting those gifts, the understanding and friendships between the members deepens.

One of the reasons why hospitality is such an important part of intercultural gift exchange is that God can use it to sanctify us. To say hospitality is a gift is not to say it is easy, as anyone who has had long-staying guests can testify. It can be a confronting, humbling and challenging experience. When we show hospitality, we often become conscious of the extent to which we like everything in our domain to be as we like it – our desire, in other words, for control. Who we count as insiders and who we count as outsiders is thrown into stark relief by offers of hospitality.

An example of this comes from the church where I was formerly vicar. Our neighbouring mosque wanted to join us for a Sunday service after the Easter bombings in Colombo, Sri Lanka, as a sign of solidarity. I was immensely touched by their courage and compassion. But the grumblings I heard among our congregation afterwards suggested that, for them, a boundary had been crossed. Noticing exactly who we are willing to share fellowship with and who we would rather turn away, in the light of Jesus' scandalous hospitality, is undoubtedly an important part of our discipleship as well as our journey towards interculturalism.

When we receive hospitality, there is also the uncomfortable sensation of not being able to 'call the shots'. How we spend time, what we talk about and listen to and what we eat are more likely to reflect the host's 'way of doing things' than ours. Importantly, being weaned from our illusions of control through hospitality not only allows us to better make space for the other – it also helps us make room for God. For if our primordial sin is to seek control separately from God, then the looser we hold the reins in order to love our neighbour, the more easily we can also surrender to the Holy Spirit.

Given that a common definition of culture is 'the way we do things round here', there is a sense of cultural exchange in all acts of hospitality. Because, whether we are giving or receiving hospitality, we are confronted with the reality that not everyone does things the way we do 'around here', and that to love them well, there must be some sacrifice of our ego and some accommodation to 'their way of doing things' so that they feel seen and honoured.

But hospitality also goes beyond an activity or event; in its truest and deepest sense, it is a posture of openness and humility. While many of us would intellectually affirm that all people are made in the image of God, practising hospitality means creating or entering spaces where one can experience that truth and discern how this person at this time, just as they are, reflects something of God. It is this hospitable attitude which is necessary for interculturalism to be truly transformative rather than tokenistic because it is with this attitude that we become attentive to the unique gifts of each person and culture and open to being changed by them.

Why hospitality must be theologically grounded

Martyn has raised the issue of power differentials, and how practising interculturalism requires an ongoing recognition of the power dynamics and differentials at play. But it is worth stating explicitly here that throughout human history and in our present time, not all gifts have been freely given and fairly exchanged. Not all homes have been opened to grateful visitors; many have been raided, torn down, taken over. Not all lands have been visited with curiosity and respect; many have been conquered, colonized, exploited. We cannot, therefore, be naive to the risks of hospitality being abused.

This is why, in my view, hospitality – understood as welcoming the image of God in the other – should not be detached from its theological foundations. It should build upon the virtues of gratitude, love of neighbour and of God. When hospitality is an expression of our worship of God, then the gifts we are offered will be received with humility and reverence. And when it is practised as a spiritual discipline, then the motive matters (in the same way that dieting is not fasting). Offering hospitality to achieve influence over another person or to put them in your debt does not help us realize the kingdom of God. Nor does extracting gifts by our own devices. Rather, hospitality for the Christian must be approached as a means of grace.

Similarly, like the other spiritual disciplines, hospitality is a habit. We cannot expect that one day we will wake up and find it easy to embrace strangers or even our enemies. God invites us into the life of the Trinity; God does not smuggle us into it. And, in the context of intercultural gift exchange, we cannot expect that training and reading alone will bring about the transformation of our hearts which is the work of the Holy Spirit. Confession and repentance also have to be woven into how we practise hospitality – including repenting of how we have taken at the expense of others, received with entitlement and excluded those we should have welcomed.

It is right that we attend to the ways that power and privilege interrupt our practice of hospitality. But, Miroslav Volf's *Exclusion and Embrace*[46] offers a profound challenge when it comes to how radical true Trinitarian hospitality should be:

the most basic thought that it [the metaphor of embrace] seeks to express is important: the will to give ourselves to others and 'welcome' them, to readjust our identities to make space for them, is prior to any judgment about others, except that of identifying them in their humanity. The will to embrace precedes any 'truth' about others and any construction of their 'justice'. This will is absolutely indiscriminate and strictly immutable; it transcends the moral mapping of the social world into 'good' and 'evil'.

For Volf, the embrace – or hospitality – means realizing we cannot know life in all its fullness until we learn to genuinely love those whom we have despised, and even those who have despised us:

At the core of the Christian faith lies the persuasion that the 'others' need not be perceived as innocent in order to be loved, but ought to be embraced even when they are perceived as wrongdoers. As I read it, the story of the cross is about God who desires to embrace precisely the 'sons and daughters of hell'.

As Martyn put it, for those who feel we are seeking to 'reconcile that which cannot be reconciled', this may sound offensive – outrageous, even. Yet this is the scandal, the 'possible impossibility'[47] of the incarnation, the cross, the resurrection and, yes, the church.

How greater hospitality could transform our church

What would a church known for its radical hospitality look like? Allow me to offer some initial brushstrokes to a painting we can only create together.

● Our instinctive posture would be to look for common ground rather than points of tension, both within the Church of England and beyond. Or as St Francis prayed, we would want to be quicker 'to understand than to be understood'. This would become the strong foundation of ecumenicism and interfaith relationships.

● Inspired by God's infinite generosity to us, we would defy narratives of seeming scarcity, and give without expectation of return – to those in need in our communities and to our brothers and sisters around the world.

- Newcomers to our churches would experience an immediate sense of belonging regardless of where they've come from or what they believe. They would know that the church is here for them and not the other way around.

- We would be as open to receiving missionaries as to sending them out, recognizing that to reach our diverse communities, we will surely need the wisdom of Christians more fluent in the cultures of our neighbours than we may be.

- Having first learned how to disagree well with one another within the Body of Christ, we would then be able to be salt and light in a public debate which is increasingly polarized and polarizing. By showing how it is possible to take into oneself the needs and concerns of others, the Church would be able to witness to a renewal of our democracy in the face of forms of identity politics, which operate on the presumption that only individuals with a particular experience or demographic characteristic can understand and speak on behalf of that group.

- We would come ever closer to fulfilling Jesus' prayer at the Last Supper 'that they may be one, as we are one, I in them and you in me, that they may become completely one, so that the world may know that you have sent me and have loved them even as you have loved me.' (John 17.22-23)

For our church to embody true hospitality, the transformation required may involve research, reports and training (more on that in later chapters) but it cannot stop there. Such things can devolve into tick-box exercises, even status symbols — another way of marking out 'us' as distinct from 'them'. They can give us a false sense of security and righteousness, hiding our blind spots from ourselves.

I think of the powerful line from Ralph Ellison's *Invisible Man*,[48] the 1952 novel which addressed many of the issues facing African Americans in the early twentieth century: 'I am invisible, understand, simply because people refuse to see me [...] When they approach me they see only my surroundings, themselves or figments of their imagination, indeed, everything and anything except me.' Throughout the novel, the unnamed narrator has to conform to a number of identities, none of which is a true reflection of himself, leaving him with the feeling of being invisible. After investing heavily in roles assigned to him by society, and feeling no different, he starts to wonder if he is a figment of his own imagination. In other words, as the gift of his self went unrecognized by others, it disappeared from his own view.

Will you see me when I do not dress like you, sound like you, smell like you? Will my joy be your joy? Will you share my sufferings as your own? Will you invite me in?

The Rt Revd Saju Muthalaly
Bishop of Loughborough

4. The Gift of God

In this chapter, I'll be exploring:

- the reality that all theology is contextual theology;

- the gift of intercultural theology;

- liturgy which enables generous giving, radical receptivity and transformative thanksgiving;

- gift exchange in receptive ecumenism;

- gift exchange in interfaith dialogue and social action.

I want this book to be a story of hope. But it takes an unusual path. If you have not come across it before, let me introduce you to Emmanuel Katongole's work *Born from Lament: The Theology and Politics of Hope in Africa*.[49] Professor Katongole is a Ugandan Catholic priest and theologian who now works at the University of Notre Dame in the USA. His far-reaching reflections on the violence and trauma which have been a part of life for so many on the African continent have led him to rediscover the tradition of lament and to see this as the only route to finding a transformative hope. For example, in the introduction to his book, he describes moderating a plenary session with Angelina Atyam at a gathering of the African Great Lakes Initiative in January 2008:

Angelina had just shared with the audience the story of the abduction of her daughter (together with 139 other girls) by the Lord's Resistance Army in 1996. She had told the audience how

91

in the aftermath of the abduction, the parents of the abducted girls met regularly for prayer, fasting, and advocacy for the release of their children. Through these weekly meetings the parents had come to 'receive the gift of forgiveness' – a gift that deepened their advocacy and led to the formation of the Concerned Parents' Association.

When the rebel leaders offered to release Angelina's daughter on the condition that she stopped campaigning publicly, she turned them down.

'There was no way,' she said, 'that I would ever be content to have my own daughter back knowing that all the girls were still suffering in the bush. How could I explain it to the other parents? We had all become one family and all the children were my children.'

Angelina continued to trust that she would one day get her daughter back.

'I cried a lot. My family turned against me, but there was nothing I could do. I found support in other parents … We had work to do. I travelled from one community to another … and spoke a lot on the radio.'

'What kept you going?'

'Every Saturday I washed and put out Charlotte's clothes on the line to dry, and every day I set a place for her at the table and prayed for her … I prayed a lot. Many nights I was not able to sleep and I would sit up and argue with God. It was actually on this particular night, seven years and seven months after the girls were abducted that I spent the whole night wrestling with God and asking God many questions. That was the night that my daughter escaped from the rebels.'

This is a practical theology which reflects the realities of life. As Christians, we have new life in Christ (1 Peter 1.23) and a new identity as part of God's new community (2.9). But this doesn't remove us from the pain and suffering of this world – far from it. We are now 'aliens and exiles' in this world (2.11) and can never feel comfortable with all the varied social and cultural expectations of this world. So our behaviour should glorify God (2.12) and we should be ready to make our defence to anyone who demands an account of the hope that is in us (3.15).

Our hope then, is in Jesus Christ who suffered for us and was raised to new life. And this hope is embodied (made real) within a new community which, through practical action, the telling of stories and through songs, poems and art, is able to help us find hope in the midst of tribulations.

I have outlined Katongole's approach for two reasons. Firstly, it provides an example of intercultural theology – an interaction of theological reflections from very different contexts which is mutually enriching – something I will explore in detail in the rest of this chapter. Secondly, I share Angelina's story because it is one of many provided by Katongole which shows something of the way in which the African church has learnt to lament. This is a spiritual discipline which the church in the West has largely lost. I dare to wonder therefore, if there is a connection between the dearth of lament and the deficit of hope within the church in the West today?

Location, location, location – the gift of contextual theology

Intercultural theology, such as the example outlined above, has emerged from a new appreciation of the fact that all theology is contextual theology. Our context shapes the questions that we ask, the way that we ask them and how we search for answers. This is not to question truths which are core to the Christian faith (e.g. Jesus Christ is the Son of God), but it is to say that how we express these truths will vary enormously depending on where we are situated (e.g. Jesus is Messiah, Lord, Christ). Context and culture matter greatly in theology.[50]

It is important to understand some of the history of the development of contextual theologies. For although the church in the West has only recently 'discovered' the importance of context, it has of course been a reality for many centuries. Vince Bantu's book *A Multitude of All Peoples: Engaging Ancient Christianity's Global Identity*[51] is an important corrective to much Western church history. He tells the story of how the gospel had in the earliest centuries taken root across Africa, the Middle East and Asia. This is the 'global Christianity' that flourished until Muslim conquests and until Western Christendom assumed the 'self-appointed role of world Christian patron', and which still survives today in the many forms of Eastern Christianity, including the Eastern Orthodox, Eastern Catholic, Oriental Orthodox and the Church of the East.

Sadly, however, many Christian missionaries of the eighteenth and nineteenth centuries simply transported their approach to Christianity from Europe to other parts of the world with little regard to the local context. This was most clearly expressed in the architecture of the churches they built – in my own parish in Guinea, West Africa, the stone church was originally fitted with stained glass windows and a pipe organ, and had a red carpet down the middle. All these artefacts were shipped from England to this little African village, because, as we all know, this is the ideal form for any church building! All of these symbols of English village life had long since disappeared – stolen or eaten by termites – and the church was, to my mind, far more beautiful with its locally made simple wooden benches and open windows. But during this period, the basic assumption was that the missionary task was simply to pass on the Christian story as it was expressed in the West – including through church architecture, music and theology.

However, in the 1960s, some theologians started to assert that context is about more than geography, or climate or language. It involves a different worldview and different thought forms – in short, different cultures. And one culture cannot simply be imposed on another. Not only is this an act of violence, but words can easily get lost in translation. As one example, Vincent Donovan in his classic book *Christianity Rediscovered*,[52] tells the story of his visit to a Masai village where he told proud cattle herders the biblical account of creation. However, as the Masai listened, they started to complain that the story, with its picture of a garden and the command to till the soil, sounded agriculturally biased. For them, tilling the soil is the lowest possible form of work. Only a barbarian (*olmeg*) would cut open the thin layer of topsoil of the Masai slopes, exposing it to the equatorial sun and gradually turning it into a desert. Donovan followed the story of Eden with a seemingly worse one, the story of Cain, the first arable farmer, who murdered Abel, the first cattle herder. With some justification, they questioned whether the Bible was prejudiced against them as cattle herders: 'They began to wonder if that book I held in my hands with such great reverence, was not some kind of an agricultural or government plot against them.'

Donovan's book, as well as being a fascinating account of cultural listening, is also a stark critique of the missionary practice of the time (it was first published in 1978). Why was there no attempt to translate the message – not just in terms of language but also in terms of thought forms? He was not alone in critiquing this lack of contextualisation. Increasingly, the rationalist, universalist approach of previous centuries was shown to have real failings and to involve unacknowledged power and privilege (hence the church's complicity in colonialism). The 1960s therefore saw the rise of all sorts of local theologies, for example liberation theology in South America, black theology in the USA, feminist theology again in the USA, mingjung theology from Korea and water buffalo theology from Japan. Many of these 'contextual theologies' received a very mixed reception in Western academia and church life. Often, they didn't follow Western academic norms, for example the theology was oral, and narrative based, or worked out in liturgy and music. Sometimes, they seemed much too close to syncretism, merging Christianity with local traditions and beliefs. They were easily dismissed, therefore, and the 'white normativity' of theology prevailed again.

There is now a growing body of scholars from the Global South who are working in Western academic institutions (as I write, Anthony Reddie has just been appointed as Professor of Black Theology at Oxford University – the first in its 800-year history). In conversation with fellow GMH academic Dr Kenzo Mabiala recently, he spoke of 'hybridisation' in his approach to theology. Having grown up in the Democratic Republic of Congo and now living in Canada, he has to work to Western academic expectations otherwise he would not have a job or be respected by colleagues. However he also works hard to retain at least parts of his African culture, regularly making return visits to DRC. Having attended some of his lectures, I can certainly confirm that he has a real skill in bringing together academic rigour with a love of storytelling and a healthy dose of African proverbs – for example 'No matter how long a log stays in the water, it doesn't become a crocodile!'

It's all about relationships – the gift of intercultural theology

Our interest here is intercultural theology and how we reflect on, and are mutually enriched by, the different contextual theologies which now mix in our UK context (remembering that the academic working in a university is part of a particular context – but only one part of what is now a very diverse context). In reality, there is a spectrum of views about intercultural theology – ranging from a simple comparative approach at one end (e.g. culture X approaches Christology this way, culture Y has a slightly different perspective), through to a full blown inter-religious blending of approaches (i.e. going beyond the bounds of Christianity to include non-Christian theology, and treating them all as equally valid).[53]

In line with the intercultural gift exchange which I am advocating more generally, I want to suggest a middle way which goes beyond the comparative approach but falls well short of the inter-religious blend. This is about generous giving, radical receptivity and transformative thanksgiving.

However, the starting point is to state clearly my own presuppositions. So, given my own commitment to the uniqueness of Christ and God's continued presence among us through his Holy Spirit, my concern here is primarily with a Trinitarian intercultural theology. I will say more on the interfaith dynamic in a moment, but for now I simply want to draw on Colin Gunton's image of a garden with space to play, but also with boundaries, fences and fence posts:

---

dogma is that which delimits the garden of theology, providing a space in which theologians may play freely and cultivate such plants as are cultivable in the space which is so defined ... But the general point is that a garden is not a garden without some boundaries ... so theology ceases to be Christian theology if it effectively ceases to remain true to its boundaries ... This freedom is the freedom of theologians to respond to the Holy Spirit's inspiration in seeking to feed the church and engage the world. If the boundaries are too restrictive, the expression of truth for today will be impeded; if too vague or absent altogether, other masters than the gospel will rule, and the garden will become a desert.[54]

So, when we engage in intercultural theology, we are 'playing' in a garden with defined boundaries. Just as any theology done properly is a communal endeavour, and just as no wise theologian ignores their theological forebears nor acts as if they are the first or only ones to grapple with the biblical text, so when we engage across cultures, we do so within these boundaries. Further to this, Alastair McGrath makes the distinction between dogma – basic tenets of the faith agreed ecumenically; doctrine – what has been agreed by a particular denomination; and theology – the freedom for each of us to express our own faith, and dialogue with others.[55] So, the main garden is fenced by dogma (see for instance Churches Together in England's statement of belief[56]), and within this garden there are also spaces where each denomination engages in bilateral or multilateral 'play' with other denominations around doctrine. And we might also say (hopefully without stretching the metaphor too far) there are also individual play areas, where theologians can interact without being part of official denominational dialogue (this book forms part of this since I am not writing in any official capacity for the Church of England). Something of this has been explored by Stephen Bevans and Roger Schroeder in *Constants in Context: Theology of Mission for Today*.[57] They suggest six theological questions (constants) which have to be explored in each context, and they work through examples of how this has been done through history and in different parts of the world.

I find playing in the garden a helpful metaphor. It makes me think of children playing together and yet learning as they do so. And this for me is the goal – mutual learning, mutual enrichment and mutual encouragement in our diverse callings. We are creating a space where we invite the Holy Spirit to work in our relationships, knowing that he will change or 'convert' us in the process. And it is my firm belief that intercultural theology has to be done relationally. Reading books, magazine articles and academic papers all have a role, but they are no substitute for talking, sharing stories and discussing the Bible together.

When I worked in inner city Sheffield, for a long time we had a church noticeboard which was positioned opposite a busy road junction. Although we sometimes used it to advertise particular services or events, the 'default' poster which was up most of the time simply said (in big lettering), 'It's all about relationships.' For a while I was unsure about this – surely it should have a Bible verse or at least something which spoke of Jesus (as long as it wasn't too corny). But it was extraordinary how many comments we got about the poster from visitors and other groups who used the church hall. It would even get referenced in PCC meetings. It was a reminder that, in a world where people are often viewed as commodities, where so much is regulated by contracts, and where person-to-person interactions can be instrumentalized, the simple focus on relationships truly matters.

This was an important reminder to me, as I walked past the noticeboard several times a day. We had two other churches who used our church hall – one a Zimbabwean congregation and one Slovakian. When they first approached us, I naively welcomed them and said very simply, 'As long as you leave the hall clean, and make a small contribution to heating and lighting costs, that's all we ask.' Thankfully, I had people on our PCC with a little more wisdom – surely, we need to know who they are, what they believe, what safeguarding policy they have, and who's responsible for health and safety and insurance. It turned out that the Slovakian church was led by someone who had been in this country for some time and he was relatively unfazed by these questions. But the Zimbabwean church was made up primarily of new arrivals and their leadership team looked at me blankly, as if I was speaking a foreign language when I spoke about safeguarding and health and safety. So, I picked up the phone to someone in the diocese to ask for help, and together we were able to lay on some training which began a process of getting to know one another. Then, when their church hosted a regional gathering some months later, they asked me to speak at the event – I'm sure it was the dullest talk they had ever heard (they were very much Pentecostals!) but it felt like an important step in a journey of genuine gift exchange.

I'd like to say that we then got into detailed discussions about intercultural theology. But the reality is that we tried – we had a few gatherings with people from the Church of England congregation and some from the Zimbabwean – but the cultural gap was just too big. We struggled to find a common language and a common approach – I suspect the Pentecostals thought the Anglicans were very formal and cold, even as the Anglicans found the Pentecostals too exuberant. I would approach such conversations very differently now, exploring culture as well as theology, and finding points of contact to begin each conversation. And I would want to do some preparatory work with the Anglican congregation before starting such conversations, perhaps using the *Difference* Course[58] with its three habits of 'be curious', 'be present' and 'reimagine.' Alternatively, Churches Together in England have produced a small group course called *Embracing the Other*[59] which is based around 'receptive ecumenism' (more on this in a moment).

Benno van den Toren has argued that intercultural theology is a 'three-way conversation', and only works well when we explicitly include God. He writes, 'the centrality of God in intercultural theology is, first of all, required if we want to approach our dialogue partners with utter seriousness'. It is surprising how often we lose sight of this in the West. As with gift exchange, where (I suggest) the only way to overcome the negative aspects is to include God in the circle, so too with intercultural theology.

Liturgy and generous giving in worship

Including God in the circle is done most explicitly in our worship. Every year in Leicester, one of our churches hosts a diocesan intercultural carol service. This was something we started a few years ago, and in the first year it was a fairly random mix of carols from around the world with Bible readings and prayers in different languages. As it has quickly become a tradition, so the preparation has involved more careful thought about the different gifts that people bring to this service. Our key learning has been about listening to people and their own experiences of worship.

I remember after one of these services having a conversation with someone who spoke warmly of how a particular song had reminded them of church 'back home'. I asked them to tell me more of what church 'back home' was like. What songs did they sing? What liturgy did they use? Who led the prayers? The emotional nature of their response surprised me as they described the sights, sounds and even smells as if they were recalling an intimate experience which had a cherished place in their memory.

Stephen Burns' book *Liturgy*[60] begins with a summary of *Il Postino*, a beautiful love story set on remote Isla Negra off the coast of Chile. One of the characters travels to the mainland to fight in the cause of communism, and after some time away, writes back to his friend asking him to make a tape recording of sounds from around the island.

Mario sets determinedly about his task, taking an old spool recorder and microphone around with him. He climbs a bell tower and captures the sound of the wind blowing through it, then of him clanging the large bell. He stands on the beach, holding the microphone out to the ocean to record the noise of waves hitting the rocks and then of 'the sea retreating'. He tapes gulls flapping their wings along the water's edge, the buzzing hum of a beehive, various birds singing, dogs barking at night and, finally, the crying of Beatriz and his newborn baby...

Burns uses this story as a way of inviting readers to reflect on their experiences of worship.

If you imagine your regular experience of worship as your 'island':

- What might you want to record to convey a sense of it?
- What is characteristic or impressive about a particular service, or your congregation?
- What makes your liturgy distinctive?
- What are the riches of your tradition?
- What are the sounds of your worship?

His point in beginning his book with this story is two-fold. Firstly, liturgy (the whole act of collective worship, whether formal or informal) is about so much more than words on a page (or projector screen). It involves sounds, sights, smells and movement i.e. it must engage all the senses. Secondly, the word 'liturgy' means something like 'people's work' (from the Greek words *laos* meaning 'people' and *ergon* meaning 'work'), implying that participation is the first principle of Christian worship.[61]

Building on these two principles, we can begin to explore intercultural liturgy as an expression of both intercultural theology and intercultural gift exchange. Let me start with the second of these. If there are new arrivals to the UK in your congregations, what responses might you get to the above questions (perhaps simplified) in order to catch a sense of how they experienced worship in their home church? What sounds, smells or sights are lodged in their memory? What did they really appreciate about that worship? What did they find challenging? Were there particular rituals or seasonal expressions of worship which they found meaningful?

As a starting point, listening to people tell stories of their experience of church in their home country can be deeply enriching. Of course it has to be done with sensitivity. There may be things people would rather not talk about. And everyone will be at a different stage of their journey. But getting a sense of people's expressions of worship in their own culture will begin to open a conversation about what gifts they might bring to a new church.

A different set of questions is needed for people born in the UK but with family roots in another culture. So, as mentioned before, children of immigrants may have a complex relationship with their parents' culture, and be wary of its expression in worship. There is a risk of reinforcing stereotypes and making people feel like 'perpetual foreigners'. But I've noticed in some of our IWCs that even where young people may not join in with the singing or prayers, they are first in line for the jollof rice or biryani after the service. Maybe such food transcends cultural distinctions and fits well with hybrid cultures!

Following quickly on from this principle of listening is the principle of participation. This is key to making people feel welcome and giving them confidence to share their gifts. Of course, sometimes people simply want time and space to observe and that's fine. But invitation is key – personal and specific, with a reassurance that you would love to learn something more of their culture. And preparation for the wider congregation is also important. Many people find 'innovation' or 'creativity' hard, and prefer familiar routines – so helping people understand the difference these new elements of liturgy can make in terms of welcome and participation is vital. There is always a balance to find between catering for the existing congregation and for newcomers.

One simple practice which has taken off in a lot of churches in Leicester, and is used regularly in our cathedral services, is to say the Lord's Prayer together with each person using their preferred language. This creates a cacophony of sound which is extraordinary in both affirming those for whom English is not the 'preferred language' and creating a profound vocal display of the diversity in the congregation. Similar to Pentecost, it reminds us that 'God talks our language'.

Many of our churches also now include songs, prayers and readings in different languages. All of these are led by different people (ensuring authentic participation) and translations are provided (on printed sheets or screens). Again, people feel 'seen', and this increases trust between participants. In all of this, it is better to find creative ways of allowing people to be generous in offering their gifts and to make mistakes along the way, rather than perpetuate a model of cultural assimilation in worship.

Liturgy and radical receptivity in worship

In Philippians 2.6-11, we have an example of contextual worship in the words of a wonderful hymn of praise to Jesus (sadly the music wasn't recorded for us!) It speaks of who Jesus is, 'in the form of God', how Jesus 'emptied himself' and 'humbled himself', and how God 'highly exalted him' so that 'every tongue should confess that Jesus Christ is Lord, to the glory of God the Father.' And the hymn is introduced with these words: 'Let each of you look not to your own interests, but to the interests of others. Let the same mind be in you that was in Christ Jesus.'

This is key for intercultural worship – not every element of the service is going to be to our liking – so looking to the interests of others rather than our own is costly but necessary. And we are also to have the 'same mind' as Christ Jesus who 'emptied himself'. The Greek word for this last phrase is *kenosis* and it is sometimes translated as 'poured himself out'. However, this translation has arguably led to an unhealthy notion of the need for Christians to give and go on giving to the point of being drained. Specifically, some have questioned whether asking oppressed people to 'pour themselves out' for others is a perpetuation of abuse. More helpful is the definition of *kenosis* as 'to completely remove or eliminate elements of high status or rank by eliminating all privileges or prerogatives associated with such' (Scripture Direct Interlinear Greek Bible App). This suggests that our spirituality should be more shaped by the 'de-centring' which we considered in Chapter 2 – not just personal but cultural de-centring – taking our own culture out of the 'normative' space and instead fostering interaction between multiple cultures.

Cole Arthur Riley's Black Liturgies website[62] contains many of her poems and prayers. She writes as a young black woman in the USA, and describes the website as 'a space that integrates spiritual practice with Black emotion'. Some of her prayers are genuine laments, expressing her anger or her sadness. This can be hard for some people to hear, so careful thought is needed about how such prayers are introduced. But done well, these prayers can interact with other elements of liturgy in a profound way.

God of Holy Rage,

Too often we fear that to allow for anger is to become less like You. Let us meet the God of the prophets. You, who tells the truth. You, who holds fury at injustice. Help us to remember that You, in embodied anger, flipped the temple tables at the site of injustice and exclusion. In a world where the powerful terrorize the marginalized – exploit people and land – would You help us to become faithful discerners of when to calm and when to rouse? Rejecting that anger which leads to bitterness or hatred of another, yet tapping into a righteous rage when that which you've created is under abuse and neglect. The dignity of creation demands our emotions. Make ours a beautiful rage.

The popularity of the liturgy posted on her Instagram account shows just how much her work resonates with others. And using such prayers in our services sends out a strong message from worship leaders that we want to hear, and receive, the voices of people of all cultures.

Other parts of the Anglican communion are arguably well ahead of the Church of England in this area. The Anglican Church in Aotearoa, New Zealand and Polynesia is, as the name suggests, an expression of intercultural community between the three partners, or the three *tikanga* (ways/styles/cultural models): Maori, Pakeha (European) and

Pasefika (Pacific Islands). All three are equal partners in the decision-making process of the General Synod and together they exercise mission and ministry to God's people within the culture of each partner.[63] Their prayer book reflects this, and speaks of the deliberate intention to allow 'a multitude of voices to speak.'[64]

The Anglican Church of Canada has also been on a long journey of reconciliation with indigenous peoples. As one example of how they have sought to mark this journey of reconciliation, an event took place at Ottawa Cathedral in 2016. The liturgy for this service is available online[65] and well worth studying for its creativity and the accompanying notes and *Theological Principles of Reconciliation*. The notes explain:

> The opening rite briefly stated the pain and damage caused by the 'Doctrine of Discovery' and named the suffering of the First Peoples of Canada … The Thanksgiving Over Water, using water drawn from the four corners of the Diocese, is adapted from the *Book of Alternative Services* and attempts to give a theological framework of baptism as the centre of reconciliation …
>
> The Bishop also proclaimed that we gather around the water 'with an awareness that even now many of our First People sisters and brothers face a humanitarian crisis living in communities where they have no access to safe drinking water, and so our journey of healing and reconciliation continues.'
>
> Each table was given a small bowl and a representative from each table was invited to come to the font to retrieve water and return to their table where delegates, at the Bishop's invitation, anointed one another with the words: 'In the name of the Holy and Undivided Trinity, Remember who you are.'

As mentioned above, such honesty about the past, together with genuine lament, allows for a focus on the reconciliation that is possible in Christ. I hope that, in time, the Church of England will produce many more resources to aid parish churches in this work of radical receptivity. But even with such national resources, there will still be scope for local contextualization with a diversity of voices expressed in this liturgy.

Liturgy and transformative thanksgiving in worship

If we need a spirituality of de-centring in order to be able to receive from others, we also need a spirituality of thanksgiving if we are to avoid using exchange as an exercise of power. The more that we are reminded of God as the giver of all good gifts, and the one who holds us to account for our use of the gifts given to us, the more we are able to offer gifts to others free of unhealthy expectations and obligations.

In the church where I served in Sheffield, there was a group of older, African Caribbean women who would always sit together on a Sunday. When I greeted them, and asked how they were, I would always get the response, 'I thank God that I'm alive', or 'I thank God that he's given me another day.' This was accompanied by wide smiles and laughs – genuine thanksgiving woven into everyday life.

Similarly, in Guinea, where my wife ran a medical clinic from our house, we would often get crowds of people gathering from dawn before the clinic opened. So the local health assistants would always lead a time of praise and prayer with those waiting. Even while ill and in need of medical help, people were willing to give thanks to God. Similarly, every long journey, whether by car or bus would begin with a prayer – usually a prayer for safety – but including an element of

thanks for the day and for travel companions. And again, when it came
to the offertory hymn during the Eucharist service in our small rural
church, the practice was for everyone to come forward, with dancing,
singing and clapping and place their offering by the communion table
– often a small bag of rice, peanuts or fruit, and only occasionally a
small amount of money.

Walter Brueggemann[66] has recently produced an excellent resource on
the Book of Psalms, analysing both psalms of lament and thanksgiving,
and exploring how the words are transformative.

> Words of worship do not fall vacant and inactive – they help
> bring into being realities both sacred and sociopolitical … the
> language we use in worship performs what it proclaims. It
> nurtures and challenges us in seasons of orientation and praise,
> disorientation and grief, reorientation and thanksgiving –
> bringing our full attention to each experience in its turn. But in
> doing so, the words and deeds of worship can also sharpen our
> awareness of social constructions and relationships that
> undergird our common life. They reveal power imbalances and
> uneven distributions of resources, and, if we let them, urge us
> forward in our efforts toward justice.

The phrase 'bringing our full attention to each experience in its turn'
gets to the heart of intercultural liturgy. For we are invited to reflect
on the interactions we have had with people of different cultures and
give thanks for the gifts that we've received, repent of the times when
we've exercised power in an unhealthy manner, and pray for the other.

There is also an important if subtle distinction between thanksgiving
and praise. Brueggemann describes it this way:

Whereas praise tends to be expansive and nonspecific, thanks is typically focused on a particular memorable gift from God that evokes gratitude. Gratitude is thus concrete and expressed in both verbal form (as a song of thanksgiving) and material form (as a thank offering). Israel's usual way of giving thanks is by telling: reciting a narrative about a situation of need or desperation and then reporting on the wondrous way in which God rescued, delivered, or restored.

This prompts three questions:

1) **How do we encourage the offering of specific thanks 'focused on a particular memorable gift' as well as general praise?** This requires space in our worship such as silence, with a bidding to recall specific events or people; or the writing of short prayers of thanks which are collected and then offered at the altar; or the lighting of a candle as a way of saying thanks for a specific event or person. In this way 'our full attention' is given to the gift and the giver.

2) **How do we tell stories about what God has done for us?** For Israel, this was about collective experiences – God's actions to rescue and provide for the people. Christian liturgy is also a form of storytelling or drama and needs to be 'performed' in a way which reminds people they are part of the story. There is also power in hearing personal testimonies, so interviews, written stories in the notice sheet or parish magazine, or brief video clips recorded on a phone for the website or social media can help (though not everyone will be comfortable speaking publicly). The more we weave thanksgiving into everyday life, the more transformative it can be.

3) **What rituals do we have for thank offerings?** Most churches
   do this at Harvest Festivals – the children bring forward a gift to
   lay at the altar, others prepare displays of fruit and vegetables. But
   why only at harvest time? What about a 'Community Festival'
   where symbols of the richness of cultural and community life are
   laid around the altar (and also used as conversation starters after
   the service)? Or a 'Global Christianity Festival' with stories, music
   or art from churches around the world? Giving thanks for our
   place within the global church can remind us that we are not alone,
   as well as transforming our perception of Christianity as a
   'Western religion'.

These are simple, practical suggestions intended only to spark ideas
about what might be appropriate for your context. What is appropriate
in one place will not necessarily resonate with people in another – it's
bound to take some experimentation. Ideally preparation will be done
by a diverse group of people who take care to avoid stereotypes or
'cultural appropriation' (the inappropriate adoption of elements of a
minority culture by people of the majority culture). When this is done
well, with the focus always on God, generous giving, radical receptivity
and transformative thanksgiving can be expressed in liturgy which
brings joy to the whole community.

Receptive ecumenism and intercultural gift exchange

From liturgy, we turn to ecumenism and the relationships between
different churches. 'We believe in one holy catholic and apostolic
Church', we say week by week in the Nicene Creed. According to
Robert Schreiter,[67] globalization challenges us to look for a 'new
catholicity' according to which the church can only be truly catholic
(or universal) by listening to voices from different geographic and
cultural contexts. In this process, marginalized groups and voices need
our special attention, and those in positions of authority need to learn

'radical receptivity' in order not just to hear the voices of the marginalized but to truly listen and learn from them.

Receptive ecumenism has emerged over the past 20 years as a particular approach to dialogue between different denominations. It is also based on gift exchange and acknowledges the need to focus less on what we can give to the other and more on what we need to receive. It has a double dynamic: on the one hand, acknowledging specific deficiencies in one's own tradition and desiring to heal them; on the other hand, recognizing the graced potential of another Christian tradition as a source of learning and healing. And as Gregory Ryan points out in his article *The Reception of Receptive Ecumenism*,[68]

two modes of reception can be seen in RE [receptive ecumenism] which are related but not identical to this dynamic. We might call these 'affective reception' and 'effective reception'. 'Affective' reception values the positive attitude towards the (attractive/ valued) ecclesial other and seeks to learn from them. 'Effective' reception of RE focuses on discerning specific dysfunctions in one's own tradition or ecclesial community (experienced either directly as a 'wound' or indirectly by recognising a greater fullness in another tradition) and seeking transformative ecumenical learning in order to effect ecclesial change.

There has been significant interest in RE since it was first written about by Paul Murray at Durham University.[69] Both the Pope and the Archbishop of Canterbury have endorsed the approach and spoken of the new impetus it has given to the ecumenical movement. However, it is not without critics – some have suggested that there is nothing new about it, and a form of gift exchange between ecumenical partners has been practised for a long time. Others have been concerned that it is a soft approach which distracts attention from the hard work of formal dialogue about Faith and Order. Still others have seen it as too intellectual – concerned primarily with doctrine rather than practice.

But in reality, one of the strengths of RE is that it can be practised at multiple levels – whether academic studies, official denominational dialogues or grassroots Churches Together groups. This is entirely consistent with my own argument that there are multiple types of gifts and ways of sharing. Perhaps what is lacking (at least in my limited experience of RE) is a full appreciation of the power dynamics of gift exchange and the different cultural approaches. Perhaps this is one of the reasons why Pentecostal churches and newer Black majority and Asian majority churches in the UK have been slow to engage with formal ecumenical structures. Interestingly, they have engaged more with ecumenical mission movements e.g. Hope Together, which arguably allow for a greater sharing of practical gifts and have a flatter structure. Could it be that one of the major gifts of newer churches is to help older denominations wake up to the reality of cultural diversity and the need to review our mission strategies in its? On our own, none of us has the gifts necessary to share the gospel with everyone in our society. We need each other.

Interfaith work and intercultural gift exchange

In same way that intercultural gift exchange has commonalities with receptive ecumenism, so also it has parallels within interfaith work. As mentioned earlier, some have argued that intercultural theology should not be limited to Christian theology but applied across all faith traditions. Although I have made clear my objections to this approach, I am nevertheless certain that I have received many good gifts from friends of other faiths.

My colleague Tom Wilson (Director of the St Philip's Centre, Leicester) has written about interfaith dialogue as the outworking of Christian discipleship.[70] Although not directly employing an intercultural gift exchange approach, many of the examples that he gives fit within this broad perspective. For instance, he describes the approach of joint social action, referring to the charity One Roof,[71] a Leicester-based charity that focuses on issues of homelessness:

The project began as a collaboration between an Anglican church, St James the Greater, and the Islamic Society of Britain, running a drop-in meal for the homeless called 'Saturday Stop-By'. The church provided the facilities, while the staff came from both the church and the ISB. They have both worked to raise funds for this particular work, which expanded to become the charity One Roof Leicester. In the winter 2016/17, ORL ran what was reported as the UK's first multi-faith winter night shelter. The shelter moved venue each night of the week, visiting Jewish, Christian, Hindu and Muslim premises, and acquired volunteers from those four faith communities, also joined by Sikhs and many others from no faith background.

Although One Roof's way of working has evolved, the partnership between different faith communities is strong and provides a good example of practical gift exchange. At the time of writing, I have just shown the Muslim director of One Roof a diocesan property with a view to them running it as temporary accommodation for unhoused people who could live semi-independently (partly funded by a wealthy local entrepreneur). This is a great exchange of gifts – God gifted us the property, which we then want to give to a charity run by people of other faiths, so they can in turn give support and a new start to those experiencing homelessness, so they in turn can use their gifts. Everyone involved feels a spiritual or religious obligation to help those who are most vulnerable. But we are acknowledging that white British people don't have all the gifts or all the answers – we are working with and through other gift-givers.

Given the growing awareness of the diversity of cultures in the world, most approaches to Christian mission now address the question of working with people of other faiths. In *Prophetic Dialogue: Reflections on Christian Mission Today*,[72] Stephen Bevans and Roger Schroeder (referred to above) put forward a model of dialogue with other cultures and religions which also includes an element of prophetic challenge. As an interesting variation of the image of the garden, they suggest that dialogue invites us into someone else's garden. So, in this approach, the garden is less a neutral space for theological play, but rather a place where Christians must assume the role of guest and be 'respectfully open' to the other with a view to 'mutually enriching change'. According to this view, other cultures bear 'divine treasures', and 'the church itself is in constant need of evangelization'. Yet these Roman Catholic authors also remind us of various Catholic teaching documents on the uniqueness of Christ and on evangelizing people of other cultures. This is not dissimilar to the words of Max Warren (former General Secretary of the Church Mission Society):

Our first task in approaching another people, another culture, another religion, is to take off our shoes, for the place we are approaching is holy. Else we may find ourselves treading on [people's] dreams. More seriously still, we may forget that God was here before our arrival.

More recently, and writing from a more conservative standpoint, Benno van den Toren and King-San Tan have provided a model for interfaith apologetics called *Humble Confidence*.[73] This striking title is not dissimilar to David Bosch's phrase 'bold humility' in his seminal work *Transforming Mission*[74] – a phrase which the Church of England has adopted in the vision for a 'simpler, humbler, bolder' church. And van den Toren and Tan argue that humility is necessary because 'we must free Christian apologetics from dominant Western habits of mind ill-suited to interreligious dialogue.' They go to some length exploring how culture has shaped our core theological beliefs and assumptions about what it means to engage in Christian apologetics and therefore argue for an intercultural approach which looks for points of contact between people of different faiths. Confidence is then needed in presenting the story of Jesus Christ in a way that someone of another culture will find winsome and appealing.

Again, this is a very brief reflection on a vast topic, but I hope it prepares the way for my next chapter which focuses on gift exchange in public life. For we (the church) will have little to share with others unless we are witnessing through our own common life to the possibilities of reconciliation and 'living well together[75]' in the midst of so much diversity.

Some questions for reflection:

- In what ways has your own theology been shaped by your context and culture?

- In what ways has your own theology changed through conversations with Christians coming from a different context or culture?

- What reflections do you have on the way that liturgy can enable generous giving, radical receptivity and transformative thanksgiving?

- How might an approach of intercultural gift exchange help in your own relationships with other churches?

- How might the gift of humility help you engage in interfaith work?

Some suggestions for further reading:

- A website dedicated to intercultural theology resources hosted by Professor John Flett https://interculturaltheology.com

- Oxford Journal for Intercultural Mission www.oxford.anglican.org/environment-and-social-justice/racial-justice/about-ojim-the-oxford-journal-for-intercultural-mission/

- A presentation on intercultural liturgy by Pedro Rubalcava of Oregon Catholic Press. Although many of the examples concern Roman Catholic liturgy in the USA, the principles are applicable to any liturgy http://content.ocp.org/ocp.org/pdf/880-Intercultural_Basics.pdf

5:   All of Life is Gift

In this chapter, I'll be exploring:

- possible applications of intercultural gift exchange in government and work;

- a vision for intercultural cities;

- the building blocks of interculturalism;

  - growing friendships with people of different cultures,

  - growing cultural competence,

  - training for interculturalism.

While the rest of the country was mourning the death of Her Majesty Queen Elizabeth in September 2022, unrest broke out on the streets of Leicester during a street march. Large numbers of young men fought battles with one another and the police in the area known as Belgrave or 'Little India'. Primarily, the men were Hindus and Muslims.

The city was taken by surprise. We had prided ourselves on our good community relationships for many years, and even while other parts of the country had experienced unrest in the previous decade, Leicester with its strong interfaith structures had remained peaceful. Much self-examination followed.

Quickly, a number of contributing factors emerged. The police were poorly prepared with many officers on duty in London for the Queen's funeral. More subtly, accusations emerged that the authorities were slow to realize the provocative nature of some of the chants and actions of religious groups because they didn't understand the language or the cultural/religious background of the groups. Social media also played a significant role, with fake news circulating rapidly and bringing others out onto the streets to defend 'their community'. Some of the social media reaction came from India and Pakistan with speculation that the unrest was linked to tension in the disputed Kashmir territories.

Deeper analysis suggested that many of those involved traced their cultural heritage to the small districts of Damen and Diu on the western coast of India. These former Portuguese colonies have a distinct culture. Although predominantly Hindu, there are still some strong churches (as in Goa, a third district with links to Portugal). And many of those who have travelled to Leicester in recent years have come via Portugal. Some are employed in low-paid factory jobs, working long hours with little security (the so-called sweat-shops of Leicester were reported widely during the pandemic and lockdown). They have had little opportunity to learn English and even fewer opportunities to understand the culture of the UK or of Leicester in particular.

The initial spark was therefore a desire by Diu and Damen Hindus to stage a protest march regarding their employment conditions and the perceived better treatment of Muslims in Leicester. However, there was no thought to notifying the police or City Council of their intention to march (marching being a regular occurrence in India, but requiring police and local authority permission in the UK). Hindu nationalist chants were used during the protest which were highly provocative to Muslims (there are contested understandings of the Hindutva movement in India with many Muslims and Christians attributing the persecution they experience to this ideology). So, the vulnerabilities and anxieties of both Hindu and Muslim communities were heightened and activists from other parts of the country quickly exploited these feelings. The result was rioting which was reported around the world.

While the incident arose from circumstances unique to Leicester, there is much that is common to cities across the world. Arguably, these sorts of incidents will become increasingly common unless the underlying issues are addressed both by governments and citizens. Multiple themes emerging from this one example include: migration and integration (and the importance of policies linking the two); cultural competence/intelligence within both the long-established and more recently arrived communities; justice and questions of employment, housing and security; the interrelatedness of local and international events; the place of social media and the perpetuation of false narratives; the role of religion within nationalist propaganda; and the creation of spaces for mutual learning and cooperation.

There is not room here to unpack all these issues, but in this chapter, I want to explore the place of intercultural gift exchange in wider society. I've argued that this practice is key to the church as we seek to honour God's image in each and every person. But can it be applied to politics, and to the areas of local and national government policy mentioned above? My answer is a qualified 'yes'. I want to affirm the approach by offering a couple of examples of what might be called intercultural gift exchange in terms of national policy and practice. But I will also qualify this because any attempt to extend the approach from micro to macro level is fraught with difficulties. Can governments practise generous giving, radical receptivity and transformative thanksgiving? Again, I think the answer is 'yes' but only in very particular ways. So, for example, cutting the overseas aid budget, as happened recently, is hardly an act of generous giving. But it would require real courage for any government to raise it beyond previous levels (0.7% of Gross National Income), given the divided opinions within society. Personally I think it should be raised, but in the world of politics, I can see the media storm and the resultant fear of losing votes.

So, it is not hard to see why fostering a practice of intercultural gift exchange would be complex at a macro level, potentially causing more division rather than lessening it. Instead I want to argue for two particular areas of action: first, the government creating a framework which enables intercultural friendships; and second, we as citizens then building those relationships. We might go back to the image of a garden – the role of government is to create the space and define the boundaries and fences. It is then for citizens to tend the garden and work together to make it a beautiful place where all can thrive.

Creating this garden includes such activities as intercultural/cultural competence training, the opportunity for asylum seekers to work, insistence on all new arrivals learning English (and easy access to opportunities to do so), and culturally competent public services, such as healthcare (to minimize health inequalities which in turn can compromise someone's ability to give to society in the way they would like). Then, if the virtues which make for intercultural life together are widespread, there is more likely to be a cross-party consensus on what compassion looks like in a benefits system, in immigration and asylum and so on. I believe this is a virtuous circle: when government provides the framework, citizens take up the opportunities, which in turn allows government to be generous and receptive, knowing that the electorate will support this. So, let's start by exploring the role of government in more detail.

Intercultural gift exchange and the role of government

One of the joys of my role is that I have regular meetings with other leaders in the city and county. Just recently the Lord Lieutenant of Leicestershire (himself a Hindu) told me that he has changed his script for Citizenship Ceremonies (when new citizens take the oath of allegiance and make a pledge to respect the rights, freedoms and laws of the UK). He now speaks of Leicester Cathedral and encourages all new citizens to visit and learn about King Richard III and the place of Christianity within England's history and culture. Along with many other religious leaders, he refers regularly to 'our' cathedral and promotes it as a place of encounter and inclusion. This is extraordinarily generous of him – far from pushing a particular religious or political agenda, he is concerned that new citizens should understand the history and culture of the country they are now part of. And he wants to encourage 'good' citizenship i.e. citizens who give generously to wider society as well as receiving from it. He knows that this cannot be taken for granted and it cannot be forced.

However, it needs to be noted that the concept of citizenship has become increasingly contested in recent years. Two particular factors are behind this: globalization and migration. Stephen Castles and Alastair Davidson unpack this in their book *Citizenship and Migration*.[76] They point out that 'globalization questions the notion of the relative autonomy of the nation-state... [it] breaks the territorial principle, the nexus between power and place.' So economic life now transcends national borders and has become uncontrollable for national governments. Arguably, CEOs of multinationals are far more powerful than some presidents and prime ministers. Secondly, globalization has undermined the ideology of distinct and relatively autonomous national cultures. Castles and Davidson write: 'Homogenization is at the core of the nationalist project. The internal Other has to be made into a national before he or she can become a citizen.' And yet, as we explored in Chapter 1, the period since 1945 and especially since 1980 has been marked by large-scale migrations of all kinds, with the result that the majority of nation states have become more heterogeneous and culturally diverse. So, there is a real dilemma facing governments. They have limited power to control globalization and migration. Yet there is a strong desire (growing all the time) to preserve local cultures. So, the questions of culture, citizenship and national identity are closely linked. Who are we as a nation and what does it mean to integrate new people who are given the right to live here?

My own opinion is that one of the saddest aspects of the Brexit referendum is that we (in the UK, and in the EU more generally) failed to have a grown-up debate about these questions. Instead, both sides resorted to fear-mongering and misleading soundbites. Interestingly, alongside the questions of national identity, a key part of the debate revolved around the questions of giving and receiving – what did we give to the EU and what did we receive? (This is still a key question given our ongoing relationship with the EU.) Yet this too was reduced to slogans about how much more money could be spent on the NHS if we weren't paying into the EU – completely ignoring the more complex issues of the number of EU citizens working in the NHS, collaboration between health services in research and learning about best practice, and a host of other ways that we give and receive. For me, this was a failure of leadership. For it is the role of government to set the terms of such a national debate – and to be imaginative about how best to involve people i.e. to express true democracy.

I take issue, then, with Castles and Davidson's assertion that homogenization has to be at the core of the nationalist project. This book is intended to argue that it is possible to preserve cultural distinctiveness, even if there is bound to be some process of hybridization, with all cultures being changed through encounter with other cultures. This is happening all the time, but for it to happen in a healthy way, there needs to be a process of reflection and learning – in other words, a grown-up debate in society at large. This need not involve a 'watering down' of British national identity, or of the varied cultures of the different nations and regions within the UK. Rather it is a recognition that national identity has changed and developed as people of different cultures interact. This includes warfare (a complete rejection of another culture – although this in itself changes us), conquest (the British empire changed our self-perception dramatically, as well as changing our eating, smoking and other habits) and migration (whether Viking, Norman, Celtic or Indian).

So, while it is vital that new citizens understand something of the history and culture of the nation to which they now belong, it is also vital that government and society show they value the new citizen and their own culture and history. This can be done in multiple ways. The Government and media outlets both have a role to play in considering carefully the language they use to speak of migrants, not just avoiding the extreme language of 'invasion', 'swarm' or 'undesirables' but also avoiding lazy caricatures. Why is it that Westerners living in other parts of the world are called 'ex-pats' while those from the Global South who come to the West are 'immigrants' (or worse)? Similarly, it is important to avoid the assumption that all people of a particular culture are the same. Political geographer Arshad Isakjee has shown that applying the notion of 'community' to ethnic and religious minorities makes the lazy assumption that ethnic minorities have more in common with each other than white or Christian communities do.[77] What's more, it homogenizes all people deemed to be within the group in question, thereby othering them as distinct from anyone outside that group. In other words, the problem becomes 'their' problem, not 'ours'. The onus is put on them to provide solutions to what is actually a vast array of social problems.

So, government has a key role in shaping national debate on these questions and in developing strategies for the integration of new people. This includes actively addressing the 'social marginalization' of ethnic minorities, as well as attending to the many factors which led to the unrest in Leicester in 2022. This in turn means addressing the issue of how government policies can enable or disable people in giving to wider society. Governments can incentivize giving and receiving, for example through tax incentives, and they can create an environment where giving and receiving is encouraged, and is practised in a culturally sensitive way. This is what I mean by creating the space for intercultural gift exchange, or creating the garden which citizens then tend and nurture.

However, the state cannot *make* people be generous, or *make* people open to receiving from others. To try to do so would be to cross a moral line. Even social engineering cannot change the hearts and minds of ordinary citizens – such as the Singapore government's 'ethnic integration policy' whereby social housing limits numbers of any particular ethnic group in in an area (thereby ensuring a mix of ethnic groups). More is needed if we want 'good' citizens who will contribute generously to society. This is where I have to show my bias once again as we are back to the question of how we nurture virtues (see Chapter 2). Different religions and philosophies approach this in different ways, but for Christians like myself, there are core disciplines and practices through which the Holy Spirit produces 'fruit' within us – the fruit of 'love, joy, peace, patience, kindness, generosity, faithfulness, gentleness, and self-control.' (Galatians 5.22-23). This is why, for me, intercultural gift exchange cannot be divorced from a Christian understanding of how God has generously and freely given to us, and continues to do so today.

Intercultural gift exchange and the future of work

To explore this question of the role of government and the place of intercultural gift exchange a little further, it is worth delving deeper into one example – the world of work. In his online article

Human as Gift,[78] Nick Spencer cites William Temple's 1937 study of unemployment and the work that voluntary services were doing for the jobless. Temple was at that time Archbishop of York and he was responding to the Great Depression and the terrible sight of the material and physical deprivation caused by unemployment. Entire communities, he said, were being broken by the experience. Spencer comments that perhaps the most acute insight of the report *Men without Work*[79] was

that the worst harm is at a still deeper level, what [the report] calls the moral and spiritual impact. This is the feeling, common among the unemployed, that they have nothing to give – to their family, to the local community, to wider society. Looking to the future, the report argues that 'it looks as though some new principle will have to be put into operation, whereby a man [sic] is offered the chance to give as well as to receive. To-day it is virtually impossible to do so, and as a result he is losing his citizenship.

Temple later commented:

I don't think I ever appreciated, until I looked into this question of unemployment in England, how deeply penetrating are our Lord's words that it is better to give than to receive. So long as the work undertaken consists of doing things for the unemployed, it is quite unredemptive and leads to no restoration of character. The only experiments ... which show that effect on character, are those which invite the unemployed to give what they can for the community.

Of course, the world of work has changed a lot since 1937, but the principle is still valid – everyone needs to feel that they have something to give as well as receive. So, although unemployment rates are now much lower, many are predicting that increased automation and Artificial Intelligence will threaten many jobs (according to one recent report, two-thirds of jobs will be 'partially automated' by AI in the coming years[80]).

In this context, it is interesting that the idea of a Universal Basic Income (UBI) is being trialled in the UK (and in other countries) at the moment. As the name suggests, UBI involves guaranteed regular cash payments from the government to every individual in society, covering basic needs such as food, energy and housing and thus creating a minimum income floor. Not only does this have the potential to alleviate poverty for those out of work, but it also removes the stigma that can be attached to receiving benefits. And far from a disincentive to work as critics suggest, I believe it could be combined with other schemes which allow people to find creative ways of giving to society. So, for instance, it offers the possibility of people being able to do the things they feel 'called to' rather than the job they currently have to do to make ends meet. I'm thinking here of people of different cultures who are skilled community activists and mobilizers, people who could inspire those in prison and offer support to those who are lonely. It would also free up men and women to be more active parents and care-givers, and force employers to create dignified work – work which gives someone an opportunity to realize their gifts rather than work which extracts time and labour from a person whose humanity isn't fully recognized. In short, this would hugely benefit people who have gifts which are currently undervalued in our economy (with our obsession with the financial bottom line) but which could make our communities richer in so many other ways.

I also wonder how the principle of everyone needing to feel that they have something to give as well as receive might apply to asylum seekers? Currently in the UK, asylum seekers are only allowed to work if their asylum claim has not been heard within twelve months.[81] And even then, if the individual is judged to have caused a delay in their claim (e.g. not completing the right form correctly), they can be denied the right to work completely until given refugee status. And their dependents have no right to work here while the asylum claim is being assessed. In addition, it is equally surprising that the employment which people can access after twelve months is limited to 'jobs on the shortage occupation list published by the Home Office'. I understand that this is intended to avoid accusations of 'people taking our jobs', but the whole system seems designed to deny people the opportunity to use their gifts and make a contribution to society (and meanwhile the state pays for their accommodation and food, rather than an employer paying a salary). This stands in contrast to other countries e.g. Canada and Germany, where as soon as someone is found eligible to make an asylum claim, they are allowed to work. No restrictions are placed on the type of work.

Interestingly, the UK government does encourage asylum seekers to volunteer in their local communities. This does at least offer a route to giving, yet the practicalities often make it very difficult. In Leicestershire, one hotel used to supply accommodation for asylum seekers is surrounded by fields and 2.5 miles from the nearest town. It is served by only one bus a day. Some residents do walk down the busy main road (which has no pavement) to the town and give some time to the local library, but there is little support offered to make this possible. It is to everyone's advantage that asylum seekers and refugees are able to contribute to society as well as receive the gift of sanctuary. For all of us, our flourishing depends on the flourishing of our neighbours.

The vision of an intercultural city

Government then, local and national, can create a framework for giving and receiving, and for mutual flourishing. This is a theme picked up by the Intercultural Cities Programme sponsored by the Council of Europe. It 'supports cities and regions in reviewing and adapting their policies through an intercultural lens, and developing comprehensive intercultural strategies to manage diversity as an advantage for the whole society.'[82] This description rather undersells it – I see it as an exciting invitation for local government, businesses and charities to all work together to celebrate diversity and grow the engagement and participation of all citizens. A number of cities in the UK have joined this programme (sadly not Leicester – although I am actively promoting it with other leaders in the city).

The goal is defined as an intercultural city where:

- **real equality** is actively sought by preventing discrimination;

- political leaders and most citizens regard **diversity** positively, as a resource, and understand that all cultures change as they encounter each other in the public arena;

- meaningful **interaction** between diverse individuals and groups is engineered through public policies that promote trust, create connections and transform the public space in a way that multiplies occasions for encounters, exchange and dialogue;

- and **active citizenship and participation** is enabled to ensure that no one is left aside, that even those who do not enjoy formal citizenship have a voice in shaping their local society.

These four goals are unpacked in the guidebook[83] which is also full of examples and tips. And the website includes online training courses, a tool for assessing the city's progress towards the goals, as well as a host of other resources.

Although Leicester has not yet signed up for this programme, we have seen some real innovation in addressing the challenges we face. The St Philip's Centre runs a programme based on the TV show *Come Dine with Me*. Families from different faith traditions invite one another to their houses for a meal, so that friendships are formed and understanding is deepened. We have our own annual comedy festival, which has a local as well as international flavour. Similarly, 'Open: The People's Exhibition' is an annual art exhibition showcasing the creative talent of Leicester. And there is a vast programme of other festivals in the city, from all the major religious festivals (many of them celebrated publicly in our parks and on our streets) through to *Darbar Fringe*, a festival of music from around the world, and *Journeys Festival International* with drama on the streets. There is much more for us to do if we are to be a genuinely intercultural city but there is also much to celebrate.

Personally, I have found myself asking a particular question as I have travelled during my sabbatical in Canada: what do I observe happening here to encourage people of different cultures to interact? Most striking to the visitor are the public spaces and the way their design can either promote interaction or inhibit it. For example, I spent some time observing people playing volleyball on a beach. The game started with a group of four friends but they were quickly joined by others who had been lying on the beach. I could hear multiple languages being spoken (some of them were clearly tourists) but the only common language was sign language. There was much laughter and cheering – especially when the ball went into the sea and someone fell in trying to retrieve it! The interaction may have been limited, but at least it was happening. In other places I've observed open spaces where the design of the seating, the placing of artwork (sometimes interactive) and the activities for children, all encourage strangers to talk to one another. They may only be casual conversations – a few words only – but when combined with publicity about local groups and community activities (from language classes to dance classes) they can be the first step on the road to greater interaction. This for me is all part of the vision for intercultural cities.

The building blocks of interculturalism – the gift of friendship

So how then do intercultural friendships grow, and why are they so significant? Nick Spencer[84] proposes that the most common theme of funeral eulogies is that of relationships – most of us want to be remembered as a loving, caring family member and friend, and someone who made a unique contribution to our community/hobby/social group. There is a profound truth behind this – our being is communion (to adapt the title of theologian John Zizioulas' famous book[85]). Spencer goes on to suggest that this expresses the reality that we are gifts to one another. And this in turn implies, as with love, a degree of self-sacrifice – we give ourselves to others. We see this over and over again in the Bible and indeed, it speaks of God. In the words of Pope John Paul II, the intimate life of God 'becomes totally gift, an exchange of mutual love between the divine Persons'.

Crucially, Spencer argues, this idea of life-as-gift and relationship-as-gift is something which is fully recognized by people of all cultures and indeed all religions (including atheists). We may have different understandings of what constitutes a meaningful relationship or a family or a community, but in some sense or other, we all recognize the gift of life and the gift of the other. Sadly, wherever we go in the world, we also find broken and fractured relationships. And so, we also understand that the only way to maintain relationships and mend broken relationships is through an act of self-sacrifice – a gift – or a ritual sacrifice (see René Girard's work on sacrifice as the most ancient and common form of ritual and the 'scapegoat' as the one who brings an end to violence[86]). Even an apology can be seen as a gift, for it renders us vulnerable – we give the other the choice to respond and repair the rupture or to withhold forgiveness.

In Chapter 3, I argued that gift exchange is also universal. In some form or other, all societies have practised gift exchange (even our modern concept of contract is arguably still undergirded by gift exchange[87]). John Milbank goes further still in his analysis of the work of the anthropologist Marcel Mauss (author of *The Gift* – see Chapter 2). Milbank argues that for Mauss, gift was an all-encompassing category:

In effect, it has been asked whether gift should be raised to the status of a transcendental, like truth, goodness, beauty, unity, and being itself … The gift, for Mauss, is the supreme 'total social fact.' He takes a seemingly marginal social phenomenon, the giving of gifts, and shows that it is not just symptomatic of the human in general, but supremely so. According to Mauss, the social bond itself, the very source of all power, justice, and order, is the triple imperative to give, to receive, and to return.[88]

Further still:

If gift is fundamental to human existence and includes our relationship with nature, then we have to see ourselves individually and collectively as entirely gift, compelled to a total and continuous existential gratitude and return offering.

This gets to the heart of my argument in this book. Seeing ourselves as gift, seeing the other as gift, and experiencing God as gift – these are fundamental components of gift exchange. Yet there is an added dimension when we consider intercultural gift exchange. How do we grow relationships across cultures?

Robin Dunbar is an anthropologist and evolutionary psychologist who has specialized in primate behaviour. Most famously, he developed the Social Brain Hypothesis which suggests a link between the brain size of primates and the number of friendships they can sustain. In his book *Friends: Understanding the Power of our Most Important Relationships*, he offers a model of close friends (five), best friends (fifteen), good friends (fifty) and 'just friends' (150) and he sets out the scientific research to back this.[89]

In addition, Dunbar speaks of 'the seven pillars of friendship' – a list of factors which will determine how emotionally close you feel to someone else. They are not hierarchical, rather it is simply a case that the more factors you share in common, the closer you will be. The seven pillars are:

- having the same language (or dialect)
- growing up in the same location
- having the same educational and career experiences
- having the same hobbies and interests
- having the same worldview (an amalgam of moral views, religious views, and political views)
- having the same sense of humour
- having the same musical tastes.

At first sight, this would appear to suggest that intercultural friendships are near impossible – or at least extremely difficult: how can you have more than one or two of these factors in common if you were born on different continents and are part of different cultures? However, Dunbar seems to assume that our hobbies, interests, and worldview remain constant during the course of our lives, whereas in reality, if we have intercultural experiences, we are more likely to expand those interests and tastes. An encounter with someone of a different culture changes our worldview and so potentially our pastimes too. New friendships become possible.

This is crucially important in thinking about overcoming the divides in society. Whatever our age, and whatever our background, new friendships are possible. We are dynamic beings with an extraordinary capability of adapting to new environments. Key to this is remaining curious and being open to surprises. I think of one of our churchwardens in Leicester – someone now in her 70s who has lived in the same part of Leicester all her life and seen the community around her gradually change from an all-white area to a majority South Asian area. Many of her friends from school and early married life have moved out of the area. Yet she has stayed put and is now something of a grandmother figure to many neighbours. Watching her greet people on a Sunday morning – Indian, Pakistani, Polish, people from the local care home and their carers, local city councillors of different faiths (who enjoy visiting the church as part of their work) – there is a genuine love and joy, and a beautiful sense of thanksgiving for all God is doing in this diverse community.

However, this dynamic process of change has to be two-way. Therefore, it is also important to state that being able to speak the same language is essential for friendships. For all my arguments about the gift of diversity and the need to learn from one another's cultures, this cannot be done if there is not a shared language. Immigrants to the UK must therefore learn English and learn it to a standard where they understand idioms and cultural references. This means that government (local and national) must provide adequate opportunities for language learning, and charities and businesses must encourage conversation practice and cultural learning. This is not a trivial point, as studies show there are a significant number of people living in the UK (primarily women who are restricted in what they are allowed to do outside the home) who do not speak English.[90] This has to change. Without good English language skills, people are more likely to struggle to access healthcare, public transport and other services as well as educational and employment opportunities. So, this is not about linguistic superiority – it has a material impact on people's lives.

Beyond this, the research suggests the need for much more intentionality from government, businesses and charities to bring people together around education, careers, hobbies, interests and music. (This last area is surprising but Dunbar suggests people prefer strangers with whom they share a 'rare trait' rather than a 'common trait' e.g. if we meet someone who shares our taste in music, we are more likely to develop a friendship and be part of a 'small community' than if they are one of a large number of people with a common interest). Integration – the way people are brought together across differences – is therefore a whole-society issue. It cannot be left to government alone – but neither can it be left to charities or individuals alone.

Jon Yates' book *Fractured: Why our societies are coming apart and how we put them back together again* argues for the need for a new form of 'community service' to strengthen our common life as a nation.[91] Old ways of bringing people together, he says, have either disappeared – for example, customs and rituals around religious festivals and fairs – or have struggled to adapt to the twenty-first century, such as some clubs and associations. So, he suggests new forms of bringing people together – a month of community service for school children as part of the national curriculum, six sessions for new parents (where they meet other parents) on how their child's brain develops, a retirement programme that gets us involved in the local community when we stop working. All of these would be mandatory.

It is easy of course to pick holes in Yates' suggestions. Nevertheless, there is something hugely significant in his observation that bringing people of diverse backgrounds together to work on a specific project is a good way to grow relationships. The think tank British Future has also recommended a similar scheme[92] and I very much hope this will be taken forward.

However, Yates does not address the question of cultural differences. What happens if those working together struggle to communicate well, or have different expectations of leadership, or place different values on age or experience? For new friendships to take off, there has to be an accompanying process of learning about culture.

The building blocks of interculturalism – cultural intelligence/competence/humility

Traditional understandings of intelligence focus on the ability to grasp and reason with abstractions (concepts) and solve problems. However, since the 1980s there has been a growing interest in 'real world' intelligence as opposed to that displayed in a classroom. This has led to ideas such as social intelligence, emotional intelligence and practical intelligence. The latest addition to this list is cultural intelligence (CQ), defined as the capability of an individual to function effectively in situations characterized by cultural diversity. Research in this area aims to provide insight into the age-old problem of why some people thrive in culturally diverse settings, but others do not.

Soon Ang and Linn Van Dyne have written about cultural intelligence as a way of differentiating CQ from personality characteristics and interests e.g. just because someone is approachable and flexible, or has an interest in travelling to different parts of the world, it does not mean they are culturally intelligent.[93] The latter is specific to the issue of functioning well in different cultural contexts. And this ability is something that can be learnt, which is part of the reason some writers prefer the term cultural competence. (Interestingly, the Church of England Education Office has adopted the term cultural humility to capture the sense that, in learning about culture, the attitude of humility is key.)

A number of writers offer a 'continuum of cultural competency'. Here is one of them (adapted from the Tough Convos website[94]):

Continuum of Cultural Competency

- **Cultural destructiveness** – forced assimilation and subjugation

- **Cultural incompetence** – racism, stereotypes, unfair recruitment practices

- **Cultural blindness** – differences ignored, 'treat everyone the same', preserve status quo

- **Cultural pre-competence** – awareness of issues and imbalances, unsure of how to interact

- **Cultural competence** – explore cultural differences and gift exchange in conversation

- **Cultural proficiency** – implement changes, confident to interact, give and receive.

How we move along this continuum is central to the argument of this book. It is not hard to find examples of all six levels of competency in English history and (arguably) in our current practice. But there is a growing awareness of the need for cultural proficiency – moving away from assimilation, racism and unconscious bias and developing an awareness of cultural differences which can then be explored openly and honestly with a view to developing practices of healthy gift exchange between people of different cultures. Through this process, all parties develop a realization of the need to change (repent) and turn towards the other in thanksgiving.

This has application across the whole of society. And it is probably fair to say that in the UK, we are well behind other Western nations in embedding this approach in every part of society. As an example of this, the Australian government has developed an Early Years Learning Framework for all school leaders, with the expectation that this framework will be used to shape the curriculum and wider ethos of every school.[95] One of the six core principles within this framework is 'cultural security for Aboriginal and Torres Strait Islander children and their families' and the framework outlines what this means in terms of the cultural competence of educators.[96] Although specific to the Australian context, the learning journey is widely applicable.

The three elements of cultural competence that form the outer circle are:

Skills for living and working in an intercultural context socially and professionally.

Knowledge – understanding and awareness of the culture and history of different groups (and in the Australian context in particular, understanding that the importance of connectedness to land and spirituality is the core of Aboriginal and Torres Strait Islander cultural identity).

Attitudes – exploring individual and societal values and attitudes.

There is an acknowledgement that these elements operate at three levels: individual, early childhood services and systems. We might translate this as individual, local church and national church – or

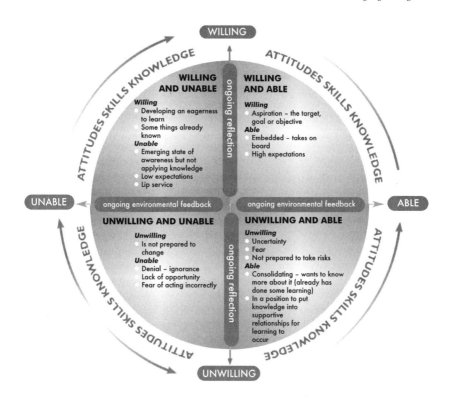

Figure: Learning journey of cultural competence

Source: from the Educators' Guide to the Early Years Learning Framework for Australia p.26

individual, local community and society. We are certainly learning in Leicester that simply applying this at individual level, or local church/community level without addressing the wider system leads to disappointment and hurt. An individual who is growing in cultural competence but finds that the system is still culturally blind and based on an assimilationist model can quickly grow disheartened.

A learning journey of cultural competence occurs when ongoing reflection and feedback supports individuals and groups to move through the journey from 'unwilling and unable' to 'willing and able'. Again, this has been an important part of our experience in Leicester. Some people whom we have tried to engage in this journey have simply been unwilling. They either do not see the need, or do not see it as relevant to them ('there is no diversity in our community'). This is where 'environmental feedback' is important – interculturalism does affect every one of us whether we live in a diverse community or not, because this is about who we are as a nation and how we interact globally. Sometimes, however, there is a lack of opportunity i.e. meeting people of a different culture. But again, this is not hard to overcome. Our St Philip's Centre does a 'multi-faith roadshow' where a group of practitioners of different faiths visit a school together – children get to meet and interact with each one, thus growing their cultural awareness. The Australian government's framework document advises that 'A culturally competent program uses (involves) the full range of rich and meaningful cultural structures and resources that are available: extended families, Elders, traditional as well as current practices or stories drawn from a wide range of community types to avoid creating stereotypes.'

Finally, it is important to note that cultural competence is not static. As we move between and within diverse communities, our level of cultural competence changes in response to new situations, experiences and relationships. Someone may be highly culturally competent in one setting while also making very basic mistakes in another. However, most groups will tolerate mistakes if they know someone is genuinely trying to learn. As one of my own language teachers said to me, 'It's better to try and fail, than fail to try.'

The building blocks of interculturalism – education

I am choosing to finish with some reflections on the gift of education because all that I have written above makes it clear that an openness to learning is key for intercultural gift exchange. There are a range of skills and dispositions that are needed if we are to develop intercultural gift exchange, whether this is learning a new language, learning how to relate to people of different cultures or learning about the range of gifts that can be exchanged (and how they can be exchanged in a way overcomes unhealthy power dynamics).

My daughter is currently learning Mandarin as part of her undergraduate university course. She was recently given the option of attending (remotely) a course which is now mandatory for all Chinese students learning English at Chinese universities. This is a course in intercultural communicative competence (ICC). There are eight modules for the course:

- Exploring and Practising Cultural Diversity at Home and Abroad
- Intercultural Listening Through Online Story Circles
- Interculturality: Language, Identity and Power Relations
- Girlfriends, Boyfriends and Family: Reflecting on Intercultural Encounters
- Cultural Transitions
- Linguistic Landscaping: (Trans)languaging as Social and Cultural Practice
- Thoughts on Flights: Travelling and Cultural Self-representations
- Employability: Workplace Practices as Small Cultures

My daughter sent me a paper on the pedagogic framework for this course.[97] This is fascinating for a number of reasons, not least because it reveals that the course has been developed in partnership with the Erasmus Programme of the European Union, so most of the theory draws on Western scholars (in particular Michael Byram's 'five savoirs' of intercultural communicative competence).[98] However, the framework includes an emphasis on questions of identity and power relations, and it acknowledges that students are themselves within a particular context i.e. not neutral observers. This is described as:

Chinese context with its focus on the Confucian concept of *ren* (任) – humanity or benevolence, the ethics of 'being for others' and 'being for both self and other', dialogue, and the ethical principles of empathy and responsibility.

Learning is particularly focused on 'intercultural encounters':

spaces where people from different backgrounds (social, cultural, religious, ethnic, educational, national etc.) talk to each other. For example, learners can appreciate that skin colour does not preclude shared understandings about family, friendship, values. Each has the opportunity to engage with and learn from the other in the classroom context as they study together ... Through intercultural communication, learners develop deeper and more complex understandings of events, interactions, and texts, which enables them to enrich their understanding of others and the contexts/places they inhabit. In the process and through reflection, learners also develop deeper insights into their own personal positions, identities, and the various groups to which they belong. They gain awareness of the limits of their own perspectives (or worldview). They begin to challenge their own stereotypes about others, and see the limitations of a 'we'/'they' orientation to the world and others. In addition, learners become aware of how language can enhance, or deny, their own – and others' – complexity, and their varied perspectives or positions (their multiple identities).

I can't help thinking that there is something here which could inform our own practice in churches and in local communities in the UK. At the moment, our emphasis is on what immigrants to the UK need to learn in order to integrate. But what about the need for long-term residents to learn about other cultures? This need not be formal adult education classes in ICC for everyone – such an approach would be a hard sell. But what if it were interwoven into entertainment, sport and art? Many football clubs now have players and staff from all over the world, and a key task of coaches is knowing how to get the best out of their players, which involves understanding something of their culture. How could this be shared? And what about intercultural learning through online story circles – a way of meeting people and making friends from the comfort of your own living room? Technology could help us greatly in this endeavour.

There are also hugely important questions about the school curriculum. In recent years this has come to the fore through calls to 'decolonize the curriculum' – a much-misunderstood term which has provoked strong reactions. Meera Sabaratnam of SOAS[99] explains:

'Decolonising the curriculum' asks us to look at our shared assumptions about how the world is. It is accepted in many disciplines that in the past, assumptions regarding racial and civilizational hierarchy informed a lot of thinking about how the world worked, what was worth studying in it and how it should be studied.

'Decolonising the curriculum' asks the crucial questions about the relationship between the location and identity of the writer, what they write and how they write about it. Would we find it acceptable if the writings and teachings on the situation of women and gender relations were done almost exclusively by men? How would this influence the kinds of perspectives presented?

'Decolonising the curriculum' asks us to think about the implications of a more diverse student body in terms of pedagogy and achievement. Because we live in a society marked by structural inequalities of different kinds, as educators we must work hard to give our students equal opportunities to flourish and succeed.[100]

There has been a lot of work on what this looks like within universities. Less so for primary and secondary schools[101] where there is a real need for a whole-school approach as it touches on every area of the curriculum as well as having implications for the ethos of the school (even those schools with little diversity need to be preparing students for life in a diverse society). The teaching of Religious Education needs particularly careful treatment given the complex link between colonialism and religion.[102]

So, intercultural gift exchange has many possible applications, but it has to be acknowledged that this is complex, particularly at the level of government policy. However, governments can create a framework, or a garden, where intercultural friendships grow in the soil of shared experiences, pastimes and projects, with additional nutrients provided by training in cultural competency. It is then up to each one of us to play in this garden, to tend it and nurture it, in a spirit of humility and a desire for mutual flourishing.

This chapter has necessarily only skimmed the surface, but I hope it has given a sense of both the complexity and messiness of this approach. Indeed, I hope this has come through the whole book. Interculturalism is hard work. It involves choosing the more difficult path and we must expect to stumble and fall on the way. And this book is far from the last word. Rather I hope it stimulates further conversations and experiments.

If all of life is a gift, there is no end to the possibilities of how we give and receive gifts. But we need to reflect carefully on how to do this well. And if cultures are dynamic, constantly changing through their interaction with other cultures, then this is a process which has to be repeated again and again. There will never be a moment when we can say that we have arrived. And the simple truth is that there are no experts in this area, for all of us must learn for ourselves how to do this in our own context – be that national, regional, local or super-local i.e. among our own family and friends. However, in all of this we can all learn from the master, the source of all good gifts – the one who has given us life and continues to offer us hope in the gift of Jesus Christ.

Some questions for reflection:

- If all of life is gift, how do remind yourself of this daily and express your gratitude?

- If you have friends of other cultures, how did these friendships begin and how do you nurture them?

- If you don't have friends of other cultures, how might you take the initiative in developing such friendships?

- Where do you see yourself on the continuum of cultural competence? What steps might you need to put in place to grow in cultural competence?

- How might your city/town become an intercultural city/town?

Some suggestions for further reading:

- Nick Spencer, 'Human as Gift' *https://comment.org/human-as-gift/*

- Robin Dunbar, *Friends: Understanding the Power of our Most Important Relationships*

- Darla Deardorff and Kate Berardo, *Building Cultural Competence*

Afterword

Jessie Tang (Intercultural Ministry Director)

So far, Martyn, Saju and Lusa have made the case for interculturalism as a valuable and necessary way of being for churches. I agree wholeheartedly, and as Intercultural Ministry Director for the Diocese of Leicester, I have seen first-hand how pursuing interculturalism necessitates sacrifice, a serving attitude, and in most instances, conscious effort. Both people from the majority culture and those who are coming from backgrounds which have been, and still largely are, marginalized, have to un-learn and re-learn together what it means to be church, and even reconsider core aspects of their identity. Nevertheless, I have also seen churches of all types, from small fresh expressions to long-established civic churches make great strides in a direction which reflects the full glory of God's image in humanity.

As Martyn described in the opening chapters, the city of Leicester is a very multicultural place. However, this is not truly reflected in our churches, where many are white British majority. This is also true of Leicestershire, where many churches in rural communities do not see the need to develop interculturally. After all, 'What's the point? Everybody looks like us!'

Within the IWC project, five communities are focused quite intensively on becoming more intercultural, and around sixteen 'Partner Churches' have committed to learning from the IWCs. One such partner church, in a rural part of Leicestershire, is forward-thinking. Recently they decided to diversify their church resources, and purchased dolls with different skin colours for their mid-week toddler group. One week, a foster carer came in with a child of African Caribbean heritage, who, when seeing the black doll, immediately ran

147

to it, grabbed it, and exclaimed 'Baby looks like me!' Every time they went to the church, this child would run up to the doll and would not put it down. There is something about this intercultural vision which is prophetic, a call to journey with God towards utter inclusion, just like the trajectory of the Bible – where the invitation to follow God grew from God's chosen people, to including foreigners, to the gospel being preached to the Gentiles, to the culmination painted in John's vision in Revelation where every tongue, tribe and nation worships the Lord all together. We are also reminding ourselves, and others, that the gospel is for all people, that Christianity is not a 'white man's religion', nor is the 'proper way' to 'do' church an English or Western way.

One of our IWCs is a new fresh expression of church. It is a community of people who are committed to the needs of one another. As well as giving practical support (as many of the members are refugees and those seeking asylum), there is also a great degree of celebrating with one another, mourning with one another, holding space to lament, carrying one another's burdens and giving them up to the Lord. This is inspired by trauma-informed ministry, and the solidarity and mutuality that I've witnessed are key components of an intercultural community: standing with one another, across cultural lines, not just standing next to one another. I believe more established churches have a lot to learn from a small community like this, who know how to cry with one another, as well as celebrate each other's cultural events, leading to relationships being built between different cultures.

Valuing the established tradition of a church is also very important. Four of the IWCs already existed as churches (of varying sizes) when they joined the project. One of the larger ones is a 'high' church, acting almost as a cathedral for the town where it is located, as it also hosts civic services. There is a robed choir that leads worship every month. Over the course of time, this choir has included in its repertoire songs from the continent of Africa, particularly from Zimbabwe. The church's contemporary band has also been developed and is exploring leading songs in a variety of languages and styles. When a group of Middle Eastern Christians were baptized, it was so special to have the band lead a song in their mother tongue. The same song also featured at another one of the IWCs for a baptism service, which caused one of the candidates to respond with tears in their eyes. What the average congregation member would not have known was the struggle that took place behind the scenes. The music leader did not want to lead an unfamiliar song which was not in English. However, a key member of the worship team felt the Spirit's prompting to give this song a go, and when they did, it was warmly received.

The truth is, developing a church interculturally can be met with a lot of resistance, from people moaning about why they have to sing in 'funny' languages or pray in a way unfamiliar to them, to not stepping aside to let others unlike them lead. This resistance can surface in conscious and unconscious ways. In one of the IWCs, some of the leadership are carrying the intercultural vision, and are even pushing boundaries creatively, but much of the congregation are slower to move. Some like things the way they have always been – why fix what isn't broken? But if whoever is used to being in charge does not step aside or raise up other leaders, I suggest that the whole body is missing out on the gifts and new perspectives that a different generation, a different culture, a different social class brings.

I often hear this comment from well-meaning white British church leaders and PCC members – they want to diversify the leadership, but no one from another cultural background comes forward. Firstly, the key phrase is 'come forward'. Some people are willing, but they need to be asked. It may honour them to be asked by an existing leader. Do these leaders see the gifts, and humanity, in others not like them, and intentionally ask? Another comment I receive is that those of UKME/GMH are often working multiple jobs, or in the evenings, and therefore cannot make a mid-week meeting, such as the PCC. One of the IWCs came up with a solution which touched my heart – families in the church would babysit for one another to enable those with young children to attend. In addition, the leaders of this church have their photos displayed on the noticeboard, and as the church meets in a school, people can see that this church is not just for the white British. We, in our diversity, reflect the image of God. All are welcome. All are invited.

Immigrants are always called to assimilate to society – learn the host language, learn the culture of the people, contribute to society. Those who do may succeed. This is why some second- and third-generation immigrants do not speak their parents' first languages or know much about their cultural heritage, because it may hinder their ability to assimilate, or has been considered 'backward' and best hidden. You can be seen but not too much, be heard but not too loudly. And feel free to express your culture but do not let it make others feel uncomfortable. Like Chine McDonald writes in her book *God is Not a White Man*, her family could bring jollof rice to a bring and share meal, but a dish like nkwobi, a Nigerian spicy stew made with cow's feet, would not be well received. Bring your culture, but only the part that is palatable. I will return to this topic later on, but for now I want to talk about the burden of gift giving.

As a British-born Chinese person, I have struggled with knowing what my culture really is. Is the way I cook the way it should be done? I still check my Mandarin pronunciation on Google Translate and honestly, I do not know the Lord's Prayer in Cantonese. How do you bring your culture to the table when you don't know what it is? How can you worship in your mother tongue when you have not learnt to appreciate your culture because of racism, or because of colonial history, or because Western Christendom is so dominant? This is not just a question for those of us who are born here, but those from former colonial territories whose instinct is to suggest songs from Hillsong when asked what songs they would like to sing in church. There is a lot of unlearning for UKME/GMH individuals, and embracing of one's culture is needed, once we realize that the good of our cultures are a gift from God that is valued, and can be used too.

But I assume that most of the readers of this book are from the majority culture. You are beginning to like the idea of a church where gifts are exchanged, where the presence of one another enriches the Body of Christ and shapes the culture of the whole. My question is whether we are ready for what truly pursuing intercultural ministry and church looks like? Are we ready for a 'whole life' embodiment where we practise what we preach daily, and not just on a Sunday? Are we ready for our structures, habits and worldviews to be challenged? Are we ready for the messiness and beautiful chaos that weaving people of different views, voices, colours, ages and different approaches to time and community brings?

Going back to the discussion that it is only permissible to bring what is seen as palatable, or shifting the culture only very slightly so that it is not too uncomfortable, I worry that this situates the intercultural church in a white normative framework. I worry that people will see someone from a particular culture and assume that they speak a particular language and ask them to read in that language next week, make generalizations and essentialize people down to stereotypes. We must move beyond a 'Victorian World Fair' model where cultures are objectified and put on display: you sing your song for us because you are from there; you bring your food, but only the food that we know. We must strive for depth, listen to one another, learn from each other, make friends and build relationships across ethnic lines inside and outside of the church. And let this cultural shift be natural. I am not writing this to scare you, but to call you into something higher.

I see some of the IWCs organically growing in such a way that the intercultural vision is seeping into almost every ministry of the church, for example in outreach initiatives. One church is asking questions about diversifying films they show in their community cinema, another church is giving Year 6 school leavers books that show the diversity of God's people in Bible stories. The list could go on. My hope is that this is the direction that all the IWCs and partner churches go in, that all of the churches and schools in the diocese would strive for. Let God's intercultural vision be a whole life embodiment, and you will see the church naturally moving and breathing in this way.

Notes

1. See https://twitter.com/UrbanHistoryCUP/status/114926970568276
3776

2. This is not an exact quote of Lesslie Newbigin although it is often cited as such. In fact, he wrote, 'The church lives in the midst of history as a sign, instrument, and foretaste of the reign of God…'. Lesslie Newbigin, *The Open Secret*, SPCK, 1995.

3. See https://www.churchofengland.org/about/vision-strategy/jesus-christ-centred-and-shaped

4. See https://www.churchofengland.org/about/vision-strategy/our-priorities

5. I am writing this on sabbatical in Canada where the list would have to include the 2015 publication of a Truth and Reconciliation Commission report which spoke of 'cultural genocide' committed by the Canadian government and churches in forcibly removing 150,000 indigenous children from their homes. In 2021 mass graves were found at various sites with children as young as three who died in residential homes.

6. As just one example of this, see Patrick Deneen, *Why Liberalism Failed*, Yale University Press, 2018. He argues that while liberalism – the dominant political philosophy of recent decades (after the demise of communism and fascism) – has delivered much that is good, it is also riddled with contradictions (not least, persistent inequality) which may well now lead to its downfall. What it will be replaced by is far from clear.

7. This is not the same as saying the country has a 'Christian culture'. I am not sure any culture can be described as Christian, since human culture, like any human being, is a mix of good and sin. But we have been profoundly shaped by the Christian story – the point Tom Holland makes in Dominion: *The Making of the Western Mind*, Little Brown, 2019.

8. For a rebuttal of Biggar's arguments, see Alan Lester, 'The British Empire in the Culture War: Nigel Biggar's *Colonialism: A Moral Reckoning*', *Journal of Imperial and Commonwealth History* (2023).

9. See the Archbishop of Canterbury's statement to General Synod in February 2020: https://www.archbishopofcanterbury.org/speaking-writing/speeches/archbishop-justin-welbys-remarks-during-windrush-debate-general-synod

10. See https://www.lse.ac.uk/cities/research/cities-space-and-society/Super-diverse-Streets

11. See https://www.leicestermercury.co.uk/news/leicester-news/world-one-street-how-narborough-140090

12. Jonathan Sacks, *Not in God's Name*, Hodder & Stoughton, 2016.

13. Anthony G. Reddie, Seidel Abel Boanerges and Pamela Searle (eds), *Intercultural Preaching*, Regents Park College, 2021.

14. Lamin Sanneh, *Translating the Message: The Missionary Impact on Culture*, Orbis, 1989.

15. See Sam Wells, *Incarnational Ministry: Being With the Church*, Canterbury Press, 2017.

16. Matthew Salisbury, 'Rethinking "active participation" after a pandemic' available at https://journals.sagepub.com/doi/full/10.1177/0040571X21 1056792 in which he quotes John Zizioulas, *Being as Communion: Studies in Personhood and the Church*, DLT, 1985 and Ralph McMichael, *The Eucharistic Faith*, SCM Press, 2019.

17. For an example of how a group of anthropologists are currently researching this question see https://www.anthropology-news.org/articles/knowing-across-cultures/

18. For two examples see https://www.criaw-icref.ca/images/userfiles/files/Fact%20Sheet%202%20EN%20FINAL.pdf and https://churchmissionsociety.org/anvil-journal-theology-and-mission/emancipation-of-indigenous-theologies-anvil-journal-of-theology-and-mission-vol-39-issue-1/

19. Lesslie Newbigin, *Foolishness to the Greeks*, SPCK, 1986.

20. Clyde Kluckholn and Henry A. Murray (eds), *Personality in Nature, Society, and Culture*, Alfred A. Knopf, 1948.

21. Anthony Gittens, *Living Mission Interculturally*, Liturgical Press, 2010.

22. Homi K. Bhabha, *The Location of Culture*, Routledge, 1994.

23. For a very interesting take on this in relation to the history of Christianity, see Tom Holland, *Dominion: The Making of the Western Mind*, Little Brown, 2019.

24. Jung Young Lee, *Marginality: The Key to Multicultural Theology*, Fortress Press, 1995.

25. Ivan Illich, quoted in John V. Taylor, *The Go-Between God: The Holy Spirit and the Christian Mission*, SCM, 1972.

26. Lewis Hyde, *The Gift: How the Creative Spirit Transforms the World*, Canongate, 1983.

27. See https://www.theparisreview.org/blog/2019/09/16/the-gift-of-lewis-hydes-the-gift/

28. Rowan Williams, 'The Church as Sacrament', *International Journal for the Study of the Christian Church* 11:2 (2011), pp. 116-122.

29. See https://www.churchofengland.org/life-events/vocations

30. Sabrina S. Chan, Linson Daniel, E. David de Leon, La Thao, *Learning Our Names: Asian American Christians on Identity, Relationships, and Vocation*, InterVarsity Press, 2022.

31. Andrew Watson and Magdalen Smith, *The Great Vocations Conversation: A year of inspiration and challenge for ministers*, Church House Publishing, 2018.

32. See https://www.churchofengland.org/life-events/vocations/ministry-mentor-directory?page=0

33. Peter Leithart, *Gratitude: An Intellectual History*, Baylor University Press, 2014.

34. John M.G. Barclay, *Paul and the Gift*, Eerdmans, 2015.

35. Marcel Mauss, *The Gift: The Form and Reason for Exchange in Archaic Societies*, Routledge, 1925.

36. Jacques Derrida, *Given Time: I. Counterfeit Money*, University of Chicago Press, 1992.

37. John Milbank, 'Can a gift be given?', *Modern Theology* 11:1 (1995).

38. See https://www.researchgate.net/publication/229846794_Praying_the_Lord%27s_Prayer_in_a_Global_Economic_Era

39. Al Barrett, *Interrupting the Church's Flow: A radically receptive political theology in the urban margins*, SCM, 2020.

40. Al Barrett, Ruth Harley, *Being Interrupted: Reimagining the Church's Mission from the Outside*, In, SCM, 2020.

41. Sam Wells, *Incarnational Mission: Being with the World*, Canterbury Press, 2018.

42. Anthony Reddie, *Is God Colour-Blind? Insights from Black Theology for Christian Ministry*, SPCK, 2020.

43. Henri Nouwen, *With Burning Hearts: A Meditation on the Eucharistic Life*, Orbis, 1994.

44. See Nathan Katz, *Who are the Jews of India?*, University of California Press, 2000; James Massey, *Roots of Dalit History, Christianity, Theology, and Spirituality*, ISPCK, 1996.

45. Christine Pohl, *Making Room: Recovering Hospitality as a Christian Tradition*, Eerdmans, 1999.

46. Miroslav Volf, *Exclusion and Embrace: Theological Exploration of Identity, Otherness and Reconciliation*, Abingdon Press, 1997.

47. Alexander Schmemann, *Great Lent: Journey to Pascha*, SPCK, 1974.

48. Ralph Ellison, *Invisible Man*, Penguin, 1952.

49. Emmanuel Katongole, *Born from Lament: The Theology and Politics of Hope in Africa*, Eerdmans, 2017.

50. For a good introduction to contextual theology see http://www.philipgibbs.org/pdfs/Encountering%20Difference.%20Verbum%2054.1%202013,%20pp.%2075-89.pdf; Robert Schreiter, *Constructing Local Theologies*, Orbis, 1985; Laurie Green, *Let's Do Theology: Resources for Contextual Theology*, Mowbray, 2009; Stephen Bevans, *Models of Contextual Theology*, Orbit, 2002; Stephen Bevans and Katalina Tahaafe-Williams (eds), *Contextual Theology for the Twenty-first Century*, Pickwick, 2011.

51. Vince Bantu, *A Multitude of All Peoples: Engaging Ancient Christianity's Global Identity*, IVP, 2020.

52. Vincent Donovan, *Christianity Rediscovered: An Epistle from the Masai*, Fides, 1978.

53. See Mark Cartledge and David Cheetham, *Intercultural Theology: Approaches and Themes*, SCM, 2011. And this website has a long list of resources https://interculturaltheology.com/intercultural-theology-a-reader/

54. Colin Gunton, *Dogma, the Church and the Task of Theology* in Victor Pfitzner and Hilary Regan, *The Task of Theology Today: Doctrines and Dogmas*, Eerdmans, 1998.

55. Alastair McGrath, *The Genesis of Doctrine*, Eerdmans, 1990.

56. See https://cte.org.uk/about/about-cte/basis-of-cte/

57. Stephen Bevans and Roger Schroeder in Constants in Context: *Theology of Mission for Today,* Orbit, 2004.

58. See https://difference.rln.global

59. See https://cte.org.uk/about/ecumenism-explained/receptive-ecumenism/course-embracing-the-other/

60. Stephen Burns, *Liturgy*, SCM, 2018.

61. This meaning of liturgy is contested – see https://www.churchofengland.org/sites/default/files/2018-10/gs1651-transforming-worship-living-the-new-creation.pdf p11. However, the principles of participation and multi-sensory worship remain important if complex.

62. See https://colearthurriley.com/writing/project-one-64g3t

63. See https://www.anglican.org.nz/About/History

64. See https://anglicanprayerbook.nz

65. See https://www.anglican.ca/wp-content/uploads/Ottawa_RITE-of-RR_2016_1.pdf

66. Walter Brueggemann and Davis Hankins, *Our Hearts Wait:Worshiping through Praise and Lament in the Psalms*, Westminster John Knox, 2022.

67. Robert J. Schreiter, *The New Catholicity:Theology between the Global and the Local*, Orbis, 1997.

68. See https://brill.com/view/journals/ecso/17/1/article-p7_7.xml?language=en

69. Paul Murray (ed.), *Receptive Ecumenism and the Call to Catholic Learning: Exploring a Way for Contemporary Ecumenism*, OUP, 2009.

70. Tom Wilson, *Hospitality, Service, Proclamation*, SCM, 2019.

71. See https://www.oneroof.org.uk

72. Stephen Bevans and Roger Schroeder, *Prophetic Dialogue: Reflections on Christian Mission*, Orbis, 2011.

73. Benno van den Toren and King-San Tan, *Humble Confidence: A model for interfaith apologetics*, IVP, 2022.

74. David Bosch, *Transforming Mission: Paradigm Shifts in the Theology of Mission*, Orbis, 1991.

75. The strapline of the St Philips Centre in Leicester https://www.stphilipscentre.co.uk

76. Stephen Castles and Alastair Davidson, *Citizenship and Migration*, Routledge, 2000.

77. See https://theconversation.com/why-there-is-no-such-thing-as-the-muslim-community-33862

78. Nick Spencer, Human as Gift https://comment.org/human-as-gift/

79. See https://www.goodreads.com/book/show/19525043-men-without-work

80. See https://www.goldmansachs.com/intelligence/pages/generative-ai-could-raise-global-gdp-by-7-percent.html

81. See https://www.gov.uk/government/publications/handling-applications-for-permission-to-take-employment-instruction/permission-to-work-and-volunteering-for-asylum-seekers-accessible

82. See https://www.coe.int/en/web/interculturalcities/about

83. See https://rm.coe.int/168048da42

84. Nick Spencer, *Human as Gift* https://comment.org/human-as-gift/

85. John Zizioulas, *Being as Communion: Studies in Personhood and the Church*, DLT, 1985

86. René Girard, *Violence and the Sacred*, Johns Hopkins University Press, 1977.

87. See Charles Eisenstein, *Sacred Economics: Money, Gift and Society in the Age of Transition*, North Atlantic Books, 2021.

88. John Milbank, *The Universality of the Gift*, https://comment.org/the-universality-of-the-gift/

89. Robin Dunbar, *Friends: Understanding the Power of our Most Important Relationships*, Little Brown, 2021.

90. The 2021 census showed that 1.5% of the population (880,000) could not speak English well, and 0.3%, (161,000) of the overall population could not speak English at all. See https://www.ons.gov.uk/

91. Jon Yates, *Fractured:Why our societies are coming apart and how we put them back together again*, Harper North, 2021.

92. See https://www.britishfuture.org/wp-content/uploads/2020/08/Final-report.National-Conversation.17.9.18.pdf

93. Soon Ang and Linn Van Dyne, *Handbook of Cultural Intelligence*, Taylor & Francis, 2015.

94. Adapted from https://www.toughconvos.com/post/what-is-the-difference-between-cultural-intelligence-and-cultural-competence

95. See https://www.dss.gov.au/sites/default/files/documents/05_2015/educators_guide_to_the_early_years_learning_framework_for_australia.pdf

96. As I write, a referendum in Australia regarding official recognition of Aboriginal and Torres Strait Islander in the constitution has revealed that this is still very much a contested area.

97. See https://dokumen.tips/documents/d23-rich-ed-pedagogic-framework.html?page=4

98. See https://www.j-humansciences.com/ojs/index.php/IJHS/article/download/4093/2034/14747 99

99. Meera Sabaratnam, Decolonising the curriculum: what's all the fuss about?, https://blogs.soas.ac.uk/decolonisingsoas/2017/01/18/decolonising-the-curriculum-whats-all-the-fuss-about/

100. The Chartered College of Teaching has produced a training course and other resources: https://my.chartered.college/event/decolonising-and-diversifying-the-curriculum/

101. See https://www.reonline.org.uk/research/research-bulletin/how-does-decolonisation-within-schools-impact-on-the-teaching-of-re/

102. Chine McDonald, *God is Not a White Man:And other revelations*, Hodder & Stoughton, 2021.